Adopted by the Amish

A Family's Pilgrimage Back in Time

LifeRich
PUBLISHING

LifeRich Publishing books may be ordered through booksellers or by contacting:

LifeRich Publishing
1663 Liberty Drive
Bloomington, IN 47403
www.liferichpublishing.com
1 (888) 238-8637

ISBN: 978-1-4897-1135-9 (sc)
ISBN: 978-1-4897-1136-6 (hc)
ISBN: 978-1-4897-1134-2 (e)

Library of Congress Control Number: 2017903725

Print information available on the last page.

LifeRich Publishing rev. date: 3/29/2017

Contents

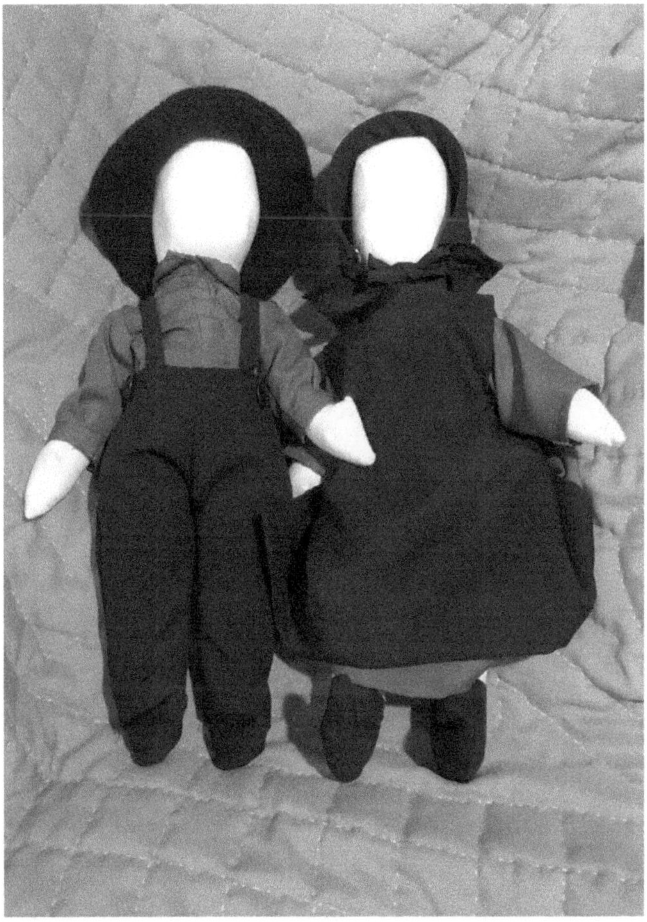

Introduction

Thumbing through the newspaper one Sunday afternoon, Bob is looking for something to distract his mind from the free-fall that has left his marriage in near shambles. Turning the page, he comes across an article about a horse drawn buggy that had been hit by a car on a rural Missouri highway. Pausing, he studies a photograph which shows a buggy lying on its side, and an Amish family, dressed in black, standing nearby. The newspaper article describes the Amish lifestyle and its customs. Intrigued by their bucolic, unpretentious culture, Bob passes the paper to Shelly, beckons her to read the article, and asks if she would like to visit the Amish settlement.

Agreeing to remove themselves, if only for a weekend, from the toxic, pernicious air that has filled their home, Bob and Shelly locate the Amish community and soon find themselves in the home of Jacob and Katie Beiler, where they learn about the Amish persecution, their relocation to America, their traditions, their beliefs, plain dress and methods of farming. Bob questions Jacob about the possibility of his family living in the Amish settlement. Jacob tells him he would need the bishop's approval as well as a sponsor and offers to act as his sponsor.

Returning to Oklahoma City, Bob and his family miss their newly found Amish friends and feel led to return to the quaint, pastoral Missouri settlement. After considerable prayer and discussion, they decide a simpler, more unconventional way of life is God's plan for them. Jacob locates a vacant, two-story, dilapidated farmhouse for Bob and his family. Packing a travel trailer, they begin their pilgrimage to a new world and a new beginning.

I am searching for a faraway place,
a place where my past is but a distant memory,
a place where I can cast my sorrows to the wind,
a place where my spirit shall be reborn,
and my heart renewed.

Foreword

Most couples and many families find themselves at one time or another re-examining their priorities. In our modern world, we often get caught up in the latest technical toys, in the mad race to work more, make more money and then spend that money as quickly as possible as a way to fill the emptiness inside. What our fast-paced, high-tech culture does not often encourage is a process through which to find meaning for our lives. Certainly many find such meaning in their beliefs, and turning to the spiritual can often assuage the void—that small, still place inside that is at the center of the technical hurricane that roars around it. And yet even a strong belief structure can be muted by the onslaught of our daily world: the traffic, the crowds, the demands of work, the constant bombardment of ads and commercials, and the struggle to forge and maintain rewarding relationships. The challenge is never-ending and for many can be overwhelming.

When Bob and his family faced a similar predicament, they determined not just to embrace a belief system that would comfort them amid the storm—they determined to remove themselves from the storm entirely. In a leap of faith—and some might say desperation—they left the modern world behind and immersed themselves in the timeless culture of the Old Order Amish in Missouri. Divorcing themselves from all modern conveniences, they lived without electricity, without automobiles, without the gadgets and toys we all take for granted. They grew their own food, made their own clothes, and learned to live within a small community that sustained itself with peace, simplicity and honor.

This, then, is their journey. Not so much a journey of miles, but a journey of the heart, a heart in search of the values that would make it whole. It may be a journey that defies our understanding, but it is also a journey we will not easily forget.

--Melissa Bowersock, author of *Marcia Gates: Angel of Bataan*

Dedication

Adopted by the Amish: A Family's Pilgrimage Back in Time, is dedicated to my Amish family, a loving, caring, and supportive people who welcomed an outsider and his family into their private, highly restrictive, sectarian world and embraced them as one of their own.

A family who shared their homes, their beliefs, their language and their lifestyle with open arms and understanding. They proved to be a community whose love, compassion and sympathy helped a young, troubled English couple reconnect with God by teaching them critical life lessons and creating for them friendships and memories, impacting their lives forever.

Acknowledgements

Memories of my life with the Old Order Amish community have remained in my heart for over forty years. I've often thought of sharing this rare and extraordinary experience with others but convinced myself I did not possess the confidence to put it on paper, nor did I wish to betray the confidence of my Amish family.

Peeling back the layers of one's life can be a traumatic experience, bringing forth sweet, beautiful memories, as well as sad, painful, experiences—some, perhaps better left veiled. Struggling as I recalled memories of loved ones who have passed, I told myself I could not, and would not write this story. After much soul searching and coaxing from my wife, I began putting my thoughts on paper and developing them into paragraphs and chapters.

I wish to thank my wife, Pat, for her continued support, inspiration, and encouragement. I also wish to thank William Secrest, Dr. Philip Tullar, Sonja Olson, Melissa Bowersock, Cynthia Richmond, and Diana Shire, for their assistance and support in helping me to write this story.

Prologue

Shelly and I first met at a mutual friend's home in Fresno, California. Nineteen, and single, with a four month old son from a previous relationship, she shared a five bedroom, two-story dilapidated house with four men and worked as a cocktail waitress six nights a week.

Shelly's father, discovering she was pregnant, gathered her clothes from the closet, threw them on the front lawn, told her to get out and not to return. Shelly's mother, who'd been supportive of her situation, told her it was best she stay away.

Divorced and jobless, I was living in my two-door Chevy Nova, scrounging meals by day and sleeping on friends broken-down, threadbare couches at night. Wracked with guilt, missing my wife and three small children, I sidestepped direct encounters with the opposite sex and was living in a state of unease. Our separation had left me indifferent as to things past, present, or future, caring less whether I lived or died.

Shelly and I spoke of life, of family, and how we'd "strayed" from our Christian up-bringing. Grandpa Bolin, my maternal grandfather, and a Church of God pastor, had been a positive force in my life, encouraging me when I was down, and supporting me when others had given up on me. I'd become involved in drinking and drugs since my divorce, lost 30 pounds, and was ashamed to let him see me in my current condition.

Shelly and I were sitting in lounge chairs on the back patio enjoying a glass of red wine and each other's company when someone shouted through the open kitchen window that there was a telephone call for her.

"I'll be right back," she said in an alluring, sultry voice, placing her drink on the table, darting up the step and through the screen door.

Beguiled by her slender willowy body, shoulder-length seal brown hair, seductive almond-shaped green eyes and long delicate neck I was anxious to resume our conversation. It'd been sometime since I'd been captivated by a woman with her looks and sensuality. I was eager to learn more about her.

"I have to go," she moaned, returning to her chair. "My son's not feeling well. My ride left a little while ago. Would you mind taking me home?"

Saying goodbye to friends, we were quickly on our way.

"Call me!" Shelly said, scribbling her phone number on a piece of paper, handing it to me as I pulled up in front of the house where she lived. "I'd like to see you again. I want you to meet my son Dakota!"

Mike, the owner of the home where I'd met Shelly the previous evening met me for coffee the next day, said Shelly would be coming back to his house that evening and invited me over for drinks. Walking through the door that night I was surprised to see Shelly and my ex-brother in law Rick making out on the couch.

"Hello, Bobby!" Shelly shouted as I walked through the front door. Pushing Rick away, she straightened her blouse and lit a cigarette.

"I haven't seen you in a long time Bobby! How ya been?" Rick asked, speaking out of the side of his mouth, pulling Shelly back into his arms.

"Stop it!" Shelly snarled, standing up, walking quickly down the hall to the bathroom.

"Hey, Bobby!" Mike shouted from the kitchen. "Are you ready for a drink?"

"I sure am!"

"Shelly's been asking about you," Mike whispered, handing me a glass of wine.

"Really?" I smirked.

"Yea, Rick won't leave her alone. He's been hitting on every girl here."

Walking back into the front room I grabbed a dinette chair, turned it around backward, spread my legs around it, placed my arms on the seat back, and faced the television – directly across from Shelly who was sitting on the couch. Rick had gotten up and was sitting next to a cute blond dressed in tight-fitting leather pants and a low cut blouse, and was running his game on her.

"Why are you being so stuck up?" Shelly questioned, blowing smoke my way, scooting over to make room for me on the couch beside her.

"I didn't want to interfere."

"He wouldn't leave me alone. I had to tell him I was on my period to get him off of me. Come sit here, next to me."

We spent the better part of the evening sharing stories of our lives, families, and our children, oblivious to those around us. Late evening soon turned into early morning. Couples began making their way to their cars.

"Mike said I could sleep in his spare bedroom," I said, faking a yawn. "I think I'm gonna hit the sack."

"He said I could stay over too," Shelly replied.

Not wanting to appear presumptuous I turned and walked toward the bedroom door.

Sitting on the side of the bed, I removed my shoes, dropped my shirt and pants on the hardware floor, flopped back on the covers, closed my eyes and tried to stop my head from spinning. The red wine, coupled with thoughts of sharing a bed with Shelly had put my mind in a tailspin.

"Can I sleep in your t-shirt?" Shelly asked, stepping into the dark bedroom, unzipping her mini-skirt and unbuttoning her blouse, letting them fall to the floor. Dressed in French-cut white lace panties her statuesque body was silhouetted by the moon.

We shared eggs, toast and a Bloody Mary the next morning. Mike offered me a job sanding cars at his body shop and fronted me enough money to rent a furnished apartment and buy some groceries. Shelly collected her scant belongings, and she and Dakota moved in with me. We were married a year later.

People have different opinions and expectations of what marriage can-or-will bring to their lives. Shelly and I, against our family's wishes, married because we needed someone to help ease the pain of our pasts, re-assemble the shattered pieces of our existence, allay the loneliness and despair that had consumed us, and dream that love and happiness was, once again, possible. But all too soon we discovered there was a deeper need marriage alone could not fill, a need which could only be met by having peace, harmony and renewed faith in our lives. We soon began arguing over differences of opinions about matters important to us. Differences that resulted in heated words, name-calling, and violent outbursts from her, differences which affected and impacted our lives, and the lives of those around us.

Shelly and I were different people in many ways. We had ignored our dissimilarities during our first year of marriage, but as we entered the second year our conflicts became more volatile. Conflicts that caused us to doubt why we'd married, and whether we should remain together. The one thing we shared--the thing that gave us hope in our hopelessness--was our Christian upbringing and faith.

Grandpa Bolin's words kept coming back to me: "God has a plan for you, Bobby. Always remember, He loves you, and will not desert you. Hold to that promise, son."

Something resonated deep within my soul as I recalled his words. It was as if I knew they were true, but could not explain why. What I needed to decipher, to understand, was how to implement this truth into my life.

It was the need to return to our simple faith and belief in God that caused Shelly and me to seek a more spiritually led way of life. It was through some remarkable twist of fate that we found ourselves turning to the Old Order Amish in our spiritual quest. And it was with the Amish that we found a sacred society, an island of sanity, and a family that treated us as one of their own.

1

The Search Begins

Oklahoma City
May 1970

Shelly, Dakota, Shelly's younger brother Tanner and I were living in Oklahoma City. We'd left Fresno and moved to Oklahoma City to be close to her family with the hopes that we could begin anew and stop the emotional bleeding that was gradually destroying our marriage.

Handsome, with long curly blond hair, azure eyes and charm that could coax a snake out of its skin, Tanner had graduated from Fresno High the previous year and spent his time chasing girls, partying and street-fighting. Concerned about his well-being, Shelly called and told Tanner we'd buy him a ticket on a Greyhound bus if he'd come live with us.

My job at a local warehouse provided enough money to pay our bills with a little left over, but my days were spent performing mindless duties. There was no future for me in this company. I wanted more.

I was sitting on the couch one hot, muggy afternoon, my head propped against a pillow, my feet on the arm, thumbing through the local newspaper. Wincing, as I listened to the rolling sound of thunder, I watched brilliant flashes of lightning split the dark, angry sky.

Turning back to the paper, I noticed a story about an accident in a small Missouri town. An Amish man, woman, and two children, dressed in black, were standing next to a buggy knocked on its side. The writer provided specifics about the accident and wrote of the Amish culture and history:

"The Amish society is highly resistant to—and uncomfortable with—the idea of change. Young people are taught to do what their elders did when they were young; to provide a strong sense of belonging and togetherness. Fully aware of the fact that outsiders see them as relics of the past they trust and embrace the old-fashion ways and have retained customs from the nineteenth century."

The Amish consider themselves strangers and pilgrims in this life. Likewise they do not believe in predestination or the assurance of salvation. The knowledge of salvation is complete only after the Amish person hears the welcome words at the last judgment, "Come ye blessed of my father, inherit the kingdom prepared for you from the foundation of the world."

I found the article difficult to comprehend. How, and why, in this day and age, could people travel in horse-drawn buggies, grow their own food, and live without electricity and indoor plumbing? It was like they were from another world. A world that hadn't existed for over a hundred years.

But today? Now? With all the modern conveniences available, these people chose to live this way? Why... There must be something to this. I had to find out. Looking at the picture again, studying their dress, faces and buggy, I couldn't help but wonder. *Could I give up all modern conveniences, become self-sufficient and place my trust in God for my family's every need?*

Showing the article to Shelly, I said: "I'd like to drive to Missouri and find this Amish community. I have to know more about them. Are you in?"

"Sounds exciting! Let's go! Anything to get out of this house!" she replied.

We decided she, Tanner, Dakota and I would leave the following Friday morning, stopping in Springfield, Missouri, to pick up some summer clothes. Staying up half the night, we read and re-read the article, gazing at the attached picture.

It seemed like a dream.

Worrying about oversleeping, I set the alarm for 6 a.m. and crawled into bed. The following morning I awoke to the smell of bacon, eggs, toast and the sound of the shower running. Tanner, excited about the trip, had stayed up all night watching television and was cooking breakfast. Throwing the covers back and rubbing my eyes, I reached over and turned off the alarm. It was 5:30 a.m.

Shelly had awakened Dakota and was sitting with him at the table, picking at her breakfast. I poured myself a cup of coffee, leaned over, kissed her on the forehead and sat down next to her.

"I can't wait to go," Tanner said excitedly, wolfing down his breakfast.

"How long will it take to get there?" Shelly asked.

"We should be there by lunch," I replied.

Finishing our breakfast, we brushed our teeth and packed the car.

It was a beautiful, crisp Friday morning. The clear blue sky was dotted with small, white clouds. We piled into the car. I found a radio station playing 50's music and turned up the volume. Shelly looked at me through the reflection in the mirror, smiled, and moved closer.

Tanner and Dakota, waving their hands in the wind through an open window, laughed and sang along to the sounds of Bill Haley's, 'Rock Around the Clock.' Shelly put her arm around my neck, kissed me on the cheek and whispered, "I love you."

It was good to take a break from our troubles at home.

A few hours later I spotted the *Downtown Springfield* sign. Pulling off the highway, I followed the street signs, found a parking space and turned off the ignition.

"Are those people Amish?" Tanner asked, sticking his head out of the car window. I'd parked in front of a restaurant and across from what appeared to be a family huddled outside a store. The man wore black clothing, a broad-brimmed black hat, and had a long, untrimmed salt-and-pepper beard. A woman, also dressed in black, and seven children stood close by.

Stepping out of the car, we walked into the restaurant, sat down and ordered pie and coffee. Shelly peeked through an opening in the blinds and said, "Oh my God, Bobby, they're coming in!"

"Who's coming in?" I questioned.

"Those people in the dark clothes! Those Amish people! See for yourself!" she cried, spreading the dusty blinds apart with her finger tips.

Peering through an open blind I found myself staring into the Amish man's eyes. His countenance was that of a gentle person. He had a wide face, deep set espresso-dark eyes and thick black eyebrows. His dense hair fell to his collarless shirt. His trousers were cut wide, made from a heavy fabric, and were held up by plain, wide suspenders.

His wife's hair was parted in the middle, drawn tightly away from her face, wrapped in a bun, and covered with a black bonnet. Her dark dress fell around her ankles, had long sleeves with a high neck, and was covered by a long gray apron that crossed her shoulders and was pinned neatly in the front.

The Amish man and his family walked into the restaurant and sat down near our table.

"See, I told you!" Shelly whispered across the table, her eyes rolling, her finger pointing surreptitiously at them as they spoke to the waitress.

Trying our best not to stare, we couldn't help but watch their every move. We finished our dessert. I stood up and strode over to pay the waitress. The Amish man looked my way and smiled. I nodded, my heart pounding like a jack hammer inside my chest.

Filled with curiosity as we walked out of the restaurant, I said to Shelly: "I'm going back to talk to the Amish man. Wait for me. I'll catch up."

I didn't know what I was going to say, or how I was going to say it, but knew I couldn't let this opportunity pass. Turning around, I opened the glassed restaurant door, walked to the table where the Amish family was sitting, took a deep breath and said, "Hello."

"*Guten Tag*," the Amish man replied in a rich baritone voice.

Freezing in place for a second I gathered my wits, introduced myself and told him my family had driven in from Oklahoma City.

"We're interested in the Amish and want to know more about them," I said, squatting down, placing my hands on the table.

He said his name was Jacob Beiler and asked if we would like to visit his farm. I told him we'd love to, and asked for directions. Scribbling the route on an unused paper napkin with a carpenter's pencil, he said the best time to come would be late morning, after chores, so we could share a meal and have some time to visit.

I thanked him, excused myself, and left the restaurant--my mind filled with thoughts of what the next day would bring.

"He invited us to come to his farm tomorrow!" I cried out, catching up to Shelly. "The Amish man's name is Jacob. We're going to have lunch with him and his family tomorrow! Can you believe it?"

We shopped awhile, although it was useless. All we could think of was the next day, meeting the Amish family, and seeing how they lived. Finding a motel outside of town, we ordered pizza, talked for hours and fell asleep dreaming of Amish farms, horse-drawn buggies and broad-brimmed hats.

2

Jacob's Farm

SW Missouri

I was awakened the next morning to the sound of children laughing, playing, and running past our motel room window. Opening the curtains slightly, I peered out of the window to see a beautiful green field across the street and fleecy clouds that filled the sky. I opened the window, took in the sweet, perfumed air and gently touched Shelly's shoulder.

"Are we really going to see that Amish family today?" she asked, rolling over, fluffing her pillow.

"Yes, there is something that draws me to them. I don't know what it is but I have to talk with them."

Tanner was sleeping peacefully on the bed next to us. Watching as he turned on his pillow, I remembered how he'd poured cold water on my head as I was showering a few days earlier. I yanked the blanket off him and told him he had better get his butt out of bed if he didn't want to begin the day with a soaking wet head. Snatching the cover out of my hands, he ran half-naked to the bathroom screaming, "Okay, Bobby, okay! I'll get up!"

Passing homes with paved driveways, cars, tractors, and heavy equipment, I wondered how the Amish co-existed with modern farmers, and whether they practiced the same methods modern farmers did. Their lives were similar in many ways, yet so different.

In contrast, I'd read that the western world's concept of farming where soil is seen as something to exploit, while the Amish believe soil has a spiritual significance and have retained customs and technologies used in the nineteenth century to honor the soil.

Jacob's directions took us on a narrow dirt road leading to an even smaller dirt lane. Two-story wooden white homes began to appear under stands of trees in the country-side. The absence of tangles of telephone and electrical lines was a sure sign we were in Amish country. Hitching posts, buggies, clotheslines, and windmills quickly became familiar sights. Turning north and then west on the dusty lane, I saw a narrow, potholed drive lined with white fences on either side. A large two-story house came into view, framed by a canopy of elm trees and numerous outbuildings.

"This must be it," I said, jerking the wheel to miss a large cottontail that had darted in front of the car.

A team of Belgian draft horses was tied to a hitching post. A windmill churned slowly in the background. A bare clothesline stood close by, ready for its next assignment. Looking up, a young boy smiled and waved as he pushed a lawn mower across the yard. The sound of the mower blades brought back memories of my childhood.

Jacob removed his hat, his face beaming with excitement, and waved it back and forth as we came closer. Drying her hands on her plain dark apron, Jacob's wife stepped outside and walked slowly toward the car.

"Good morning," she said, smiling widely, her eyes turning into tiny slits in her pink, puffy face. "I'm Katie, Jacob's wife. Would you'ns like to come in and have some freshly made cookies and a glass of milk with us?"

"We'd love to," I said, crawling out of the car, stretching my arms toward the sky, turning to shut the door behind me.

Shelly, Tanner and Dakota followed us to the house.

"Good morning!" Jacob said.

"Good morning," I replied.

I was struck, as I entered and looked around the home, by its simplicity. The windows were covered with plain white curtains. A well-used wood burning stove, two wooden rocking chairs, several straight-back wooden chairs, a treadle sewing machine and an old cadaverous, well-used cloth couch filled the living room. The wooden floor and walls had ostensibly been scrubbed clean.

Two kerosene lamps hung to the left of the door. A row of weathered coats and hats hung loosely on wooden pegs to the right. A small book shelf sat next to a rocking chair, holding only a well-worn Bible and another book. The room appeared to glow. There were no pictures, paintings or mirrors on the walls. A calendar hung above a chair.

Jacob sat down in a tall rocking chair, leaned back and lit his pipe. The smell of freshly baked cookies wafted through the house. I glanced through a large glass window and saw a young Amish family sitting in a horse-drawn buggy, trotting down the highway. I could hear their laughter above the clop, clop of the horse's hooves.

The noise emanating from the iron-wrapped, wooden spoke wheels as the buggy passed us is a sound I will never forget. Sitting quietly and still as if in a trance, I felt as though I were inside a still-life painting. Afraid to move a muscle, I wanted this moment to last forever.

"I never dreamed I'd be sitting in an Amish home. This is a whole new world to me," I said, turning around, sweeping the room with my eyes, taking in and letting out a deep breath, savoring the moment.

"We want to learn more about the English, and even though we choose not to live as you'ns do, that doesn't mean we cannot learn from you," Jacob said, puffing on his pipe, exhaling slowly.

"The English?" I asked, scratching my head.

"You are known as the English to the Amish. We speak Dutch German, but learn English so that we may better communicate with the outside world."

Katie walked through the door and left a plate of hot chocolate chip cookies on a table before returning to the kitchen. A tall, shapely young woman followed closely behind, carrying several large glasses of milk.

Dressed in a plain dark dress, gray apron, bonnet and high-topped shoes, the young woman was uncommonly beautiful. Her high cheekbones gave way to eyes the color of mint, bound by long, full, dark eyelashes. Smiling politely, her heart shaped full lips exposed beautiful white, even teeth.

"Thank you," Tanner said, reaching for a cookie, quickly looking down at the floor. Clearly, her beauty had overwhelmed him.

Jacob asked what I knew of the Amish. I told him I knew very little, but wanted to learn more about their lifestyle, culture, and religion.

He leaned forward in his rocker, placed his hand on his knee, and began telling me about Amish history and how his people left Switzerland for America in the 1700's to escape persecution. He pointed to the book next to the Bible, said it was the *Book of Martyrs* and that every Amish family kept this book in their home to remind them of the suffering their forefathers had endured.

"We are Old Order Amish, unlike the Pennsylvania and Indiana Amish," he said proudly, leaning back, puffing on his pipe. "We dress more conservatively and our buggies have no enclosed cabs or rubber tires. The Amish are direct descendants of the Anabaptists of sixteenth century Europe and were among the early Germanic settlers in Pennsylvania. Named after their leader, Jacob Amman, they are a branch of the Swiss Brethren, one of three counter-culture reformist groups."

Rising from his chair he called out loudly, "Mandy!" A young woman entered the room and stood at the doorway. Mandy was the same woman who'd earlier served us milk.

"These young fellas want to see the farm. Would you kindly oblige them?" he said, looking across the room at Tanner and Dakota.

"Yes, Father," Mandy replied.

"Would you'ns like to see the rest of the house?" Katie asked, stepping into the front room.

A large oak table and ten chairs sat in the middle of the kitchen. Along one wall sat a high chair and an icebox. To the right of a door and in the middle of the wall was a large kerosene cook stove, with a tea kettle and two porcelain dish pans resting on it. A large galvanized tub hung on another wall.

"What's the tub used for?" I asked.

"For our baths," Katie said, blushing.

Katie led us to a bedroom and unfolded a beautiful handmade quilt her grandmother had made for her. She laid it out on the bed, saying that Amish women often give quilts as gifts to each other on special occasions. Shelly touched the fabric reverently, noticing the tiny stitches.

The wooden steps creaked and groaned as we walked up the well-worn stairs to the children's bedrooms. Jacob and Katie had seven children: Mandy, nineteen, followed by Petie, seventeen; Joseph, fourteen; Jonas, twelve; Barbara, nine; Andy, five and Mattie, three.

Petie was tall, thin, and had deep-set green eyes. Shy, he kept his head lowered as he spoke. In contrast, Joseph was short, muscular, outgoing, and wore a constant smile, very much like his father. Jonas was handsome, dark-skinned, dark eyed and a flirt—taking advantage of every opportunity to sit next to Shelly.

Tall, pretty and graceful, Barbara was sure to be a beautiful young maiden one day and a catch for any young Amish man. Andy and Mattie were typical five and three-year olds, running and skipping simultaneously from room to room, laughing out loud and chasing each other around the house.

Mandy's bed, chest of drawers and kerosene lamp were located in one corner of the first bedroom. Barbara and Mattie shared a small bed, chest of drawers, and kerosene lamp in the opposite corner of the same bedroom. Petie, Joseph, Jonas, and Andy shared a closet, chest of drawers and two kerosene lamps in the second bedroom.

Walking back downstairs, we strolled through the kitchen and out the rear of the house. Off to the left was a well-trodden path to an outhouse and to the right, a large barn. Strolling through the barn brought back sweet memories of Grandpa Bolin's farm and for a moment I was a child again, running through his barn, rolling in the hay and petting his cows and horses.

Mandy and Tanner were sitting on the back porch upon our return to the house. Tanner looked up at me and smiled, his face turning bright red, his eyes glistening. I got the feeling he had taken a shine to Mandy.

"Are there any farmers in your family?" Jacob asked, sitting down in his rocker.

I told him grandpa had been a farmer but I'd never tried my hand at it.

"How old is your son?" he asked, looking through the window at Dakota as he chased Andy across the lawn.

"Three," I replied.

"Andy will be in school soon. Amish children go to grammar school through the eighth grade but do not attend high school."

Jacob said the teen years are a time when Amish children go through an important development period in their lives and Amish parents do not want their teenagers influenced by the English at that critical age. No offense, he went on to say, but, without the help of their teens they wouldn't be able to operate their farms and the farming skills the teens learn during this time prepare them to manage their own farms once they're married.

Katie and Shelly walked into the front room, followed by Tanner and Mandy.

"It's getting close to their chore time, Bobby. We should go," Shelly said apologetically.

Jacob wrote something on a piece of paper and handed it to me, saying it was his English neighbor's phone number.

"Call and leave a message for me if you wanna talk! I'll call you back as soon as I can," he said, grinning like a man with something on his mind.

Shaking my hand firmly he placed his other hand on my shoulder and said, "We're glad you'ns came and would be pleased to have you come back again."

I told him we were going to spend the night in town and look around the next day before leaving for home.

"We don't have church tomorrow. You'ns could come back for lunch if you like."

I looked at Shelly for an answer. Nodding yes, her face flushed with excitement.

"I guess we'll see you tomorrow!" I said.

"Don't forget your son!" Katie cried out, laughing and pointing toward the barn.

Shading my eyes from the glaring afternoon sun, I caught a glimpse of Dakota chasing Andy around the chicken coop with a handful of hay. They laughed as they darted under, around and between the cows, caught up with each other, and wrestled to the ground. Running to them, I picked up Dakota, brushed the hay out of his hair, cuffed him lightly on the seat of his jeans and placed him in the car. Looking through the rear-view mirror as we drove away, I saw Jacob, Katie and

Mandy standing on the front porch. Jacob, leaning against the porch post, looked to be the pillar of strength.

Katie, tucking ringlets of hair under her bonnet, smiled and rested her hand on Jacob's shoulder. Mandy waved and smiled. The rest of the children, peeking from around the corner of the house, giggled and ran out of sight.

I couldn't help but think, as I turned onto the state highway, that I'd entered another world, another time, and how a chance meeting with an Amish family may have changed my life...our lives...forever. I had seen a way of life I didn't know existed. A way of life I found intriguing and alluring. I couldn't wait to return the next day.

3

One Day Later

Sunday morning came early. Driving through the verdant, hilly countryside, I wondered, *Could we live in an Old Order Amish community? What would it be like to be a part of a close-knit society that kept to themselves and depended entirely on each other for help? Could we abide by the Amish strict rules? What would our families think of us?*

I imagined myself sitting in the driver's seat of a shiny black buggy, holding the leather reins of a beautiful horse in my hands, trotting down a tree-lined dirt road with spoke wheels creaking, harness jingling and the smell of leather in the air. Shelly was sitting beside me wearing a black cap, black dress, and black shoes.

She was beautiful.

I rolled my window down and breathed in the cool, fresh country air. The fields had been plowed and planted. Hungry robins stood firmly in the rich top soil, bracing their bodies as they tugged at unfortunate worms. A bright red cardinal took flight from a fence post, joining his less colorful mate in a tall cottonwood tree.

Jonas and Barbara ran to the car as we turned into the drive. Jonas was shoeless, and wore loose pants that were held up by plain gray suspenders. He had on a tattered white shirt and wore a floppy weathered straw hat.

Barbara's hair was parted in the middle, drawn tightly backward in a bun and covered with a loose-fitting white cap. She wore a light-colored, full-bodied dress and her tiny, white feet were bare. Grinning playfully at Tanner, she tapped on the back window of the car, giggled, and ran away. Jonas, watching as she ran to the barn, turned and chased after her.

"C'mon in!" Katie shouted, opening the front door of the house.

Jacob and Mandy greeted us at the front door. Katie asked Shelly if she'd like to sit with her in the kitchen while she and Mandy made lunch.

I couldn't help but feel the presence of someone watching me as I leaned back on the well-worn, cloth brown couch. Smiling slyly out of the corner of his mouth, Jacob slowly placed his pipe on the table and pointed covertly at the window behind me. Attempting not to give myself away I turned to see Andy and Mattie: their tiny, freckled noses pressed against the glass, their hands wrapped around their eyes, as if looking into a submarine periscope, studying me.

"Boo!" I shouted, jumping to my feet, walking swiftly to the front door.

Scurrying off the porch, screaming at the top of their voices, they ran to the barn as fast as their little legs could carry them.

"Come have a bowl of soup and bread with us," Katie said, stepping into the front room.

"Yes, please come eat with us," Jacob said, rising from his chair, stretching as he walked to the kitchen.

I quickly realized, upon entering the kitchen, that each family member had assigned places and tasks. Jacob, standing at the far end of the table, pulled four chairs back and asked Shelly, Tanner, Dakota, and me to please sit. Walking back to the head of the table he sat, smiled graciously, and waited. The boys, youngest to oldest, sat to his right. Katie sat to his left. The youngest daughter sat next to Katie, followed by the next in age, and so on.

Rising from her chair and walking to the stove, Katie filled large glass bowls with fresh vegetable soup and set each bowl on a plate. Mandy spread freshly churned butter on warm slices of bread and placed a large pitcher of milk on the table.

Finished with their tasks, Katie and Mandy pulled their chairs back and sat down quietly. Family members clasped their hands under their chins, bowed quietly and whispered a private prayer. Taking their cue, Shelly, Tanner, Dakota and I lowered our heads and prayed under our breath.

"Well then, reach in and help yourselves!" Jacob said loudly.

Filling our plates, we ate our meal quietly and without much ado. Mandy and Katie cleared the table and hand-washed the dishes. Their movements, swift, organized, and deliberate were the epitome of efficiency and organization.

Katie and Shelly stayed in the kitchen after the dishes were finished. Mandy invited Tanner to go with her to the barn to check on a mare that'd been ill. Dakota and Andy followed closely behind. Jacob and I returned to the front room.

"What caused the Missouri Amish to leave Indiana?" I asked.

"There had been continual strife and bickering in the community regarding differences of opinion and conformity to our strict Amish ways. Some Amish live by conservative standards, while others prefer a more modern discipline. Others who left were seeking new settlements to escape church problems, improve youth standards, and avoid over-crowding. After looking at farms in Missouri, more than twenty families left Indiana and moved here in 1968. We bought run-down farms and worked hard to make them productive. What line of work are you in?" he asked.

Had he somehow over-heard my thoughts? Read my mind, I wondered.

"I've painted, loaded box cars, pumped gas and am currently working in a warehouse."

"Would you like to take a walk?" he asked, rising from his chair, reaching for his hat.

I felt a sense of tranquility as we strode through the farm. It felt good, and somewhat natural, to be back among the Amish.

"Have you ever thought about living and working on a farm?" Jacob asked, pointing at a farmer across the road, driving a team of horses.

"I've always wanted to try farming, but have never plowed a field or planted a garden," I mused. "I don't think I'd be much of a hand at farming," I laughed.

"Have you done any carpentry work?" he pursued.

"I helped my brother-in-law build a garage once. It wasn't as hard as I thought it would be. I'm a quick learner!"

I asked if it would be possible for an English family to live in an Amish community. He said it could be, but that I'd have to have an Amish sponsor and the bishop's approval. He explained that the bishop was the local congregation leader and administered rites, acceptances, and excommunications.

"Each Amish district is different. One bishop may allow an English family to join its community, while most would not, I reckon."

Jacob explained, "Our day typically starts at five a.m. milking cows, feeding farm animals and performing other chores. During the busy season we plow, seed, and harvest until late in the evening. The women keep the gardens and milk the cows."

"Could an English family living here have a small farm and garden?" I asked.

"You could have a garden big enough for your small family and work with some of the Amish men who do construction work for the English. Do you think your wife would like living with the Amish?" he continued, turning back toward the house.

"I don't know. I'd have to talk to her and see how she feels about it."

"And Tanner?" he asked.

"Tanner plans to go to college in Oklahoma City this fall."

I hesitated for a moment. Summoning the courage, I asked if he would be willing to sponsor me if we decided to move to Missouri.

"I'd be happy to be your sponsor and welcome you to the Amish community," he said, appearing to be pleased I'd asked.

We walked back to the house, entered the kitchen and found Katie and Shelly sitting around a quilt Katie had spread out on the table. Katie was explaining to Shelly how Amish quilts were made. Mandy, Tanner, Andy, and Dakota were eating popcorn and drinking hot chocolate topped with melted marshmallows.

"American women were making quilts in the 1700s," she said. "The earliest known quilts made by the Amish were in 1831, in Ohio. Amish women adopted quilting styles and made them in strong, unprinted colors. We adopted our own styles and techniques of quilt making and took those styles with us as we formed new settlements. Not everyone agrees on which colors are acceptable. The Old Order settlements, such as we are, choose darker colors over the lighter colors of the New Order settlements."

I whispered to Shelly that we had a long drive ahead of us and said we'd better get on the road soon. Thanking Jacob and Katie for their hospitality, we walked outside, gathered up our family and climbed into the car.

"We hope to see you'ns again," Jacob shouted as we drove away.

It was quiet as we left the farm, drove down the dirt road and onto the state highway. Thoughts of Jacob, Katie, the children and how much we had enjoyed our visit filled my head as I looked out through the bug-spattered windshield. Shelly leaned her head against the window and gazed out at the open fields. Tanner and Dakota sat motionless in the rear seat, peering through the windows.

"I miss Andy," Dakota said mournfully, wiping a singular tear from his eye. "Can I come see him again?"

"Would you like that?" Shelly asked, turning around, raising up his chin.

"Yes, he's my friend. We had fun together."

"Did you have a good time?" Shelly asked Tanner.

"Yes. I really like Mandy. She's not like the girls in Oklahoma City, or in California. She's different."

I told them what I'd learned about the Amish faith and how they farmed their land. Shelly said she enjoyed her visit with Katie and Mandy and that they'd talked about quilting, making their own clothing, gardening and canning.

"I helped milk a cow!" Dakota cried out, smiling widely through his tears.

"And I got to help Mandy take care of a sick horse," Tanner said proudly, reflecting on the time they'd spent together.

"Mom, can we have a cow?" Dakota asked.

"No, honey. We don't have a place to put a cow."

"I like milking cows," Dakota replied. "And guess what, I got to drink cow's milk!"

"You did?" Shelly exclaimed.

"Yes! And it was warm, and sweet, and good!"

"Do the Amish go to college?" Tanner asked.

"No. Their education stops at the eighth grade," I replied.

"Then how do they support their families?" he questioned.

"They raise and can their own food and make their own clothes. They don't pay for electricity, they don't own a car, or need gasoline, or maintenance for one, and they help each other when they need a house or a barn built."

"Cool!" Dakota shouted.

Quietness filled the car. I turned on the radio and returned to my thoughts.

Could the Amish be the answer to our prayers, I wondered.

We stopped for a restroom break in Joplin, had a quick snack, arrived safely at home in time to unpack the car and retire for the evening.

Lying in bed that evening, staring at the ceiling with my hands folded behind my head, I thought of how much I missed my children in California, of how Shelly and I were slowly drifting apart, and of the opportunity we had to do something special with our lives.

"Do you miss going to church?" Shelly asked, rolling over, placing her head on my shoulder.

"Yes."

"Katie and I talked about our problems."

"What problems?" I asked, concerned she had shared our marital problems with Katie.

"You know, fighting all the time. We talked about our marriage, the Amish, families and church."

"What did you tell her?"

"I told her we argue a lot, that we'd strayed from church, and how I was afraid we were going to wind up divorced if we didn't stop fighting."

"What did she say?"

"She said maybe we should think about getting back in church and getting our lives straightened out. She said the Amish don't believe in divorce. I really like Katie. She treats me like a sister."

"Jacob's pretty cool, too. I learned a lot from him. We'd better get some sleep," I said, reaching over, kissing her.

"Good night," she said, rolling over, tucking the covers under her chin.

4

Decisions

Two weeks had passed since we first met Jacob, Katie and their family. I couldn't get them off my mind. My days and nights were spent wondering what they were doing and if they ever thought about us.

Sipping on a cup of coffee one Saturday morning, trying to get my eyes focused and my brain in gear, I was feeling forlorn, and wondered what I could do to get myself out of the doldrums. The lawn needed mowing, the bathroom sink had sprung a leak, but my mind kept drifting back to Jacob and the farm.

Shelly came to the table, poured herself a cup of coffee and sat down next to me.

"I miss Katie," she said longingly. "I want to learn how to sew and quilt and grow a garden the way she does. She said she'd teach me. Do you ever think about Jacob?" she asked, looking out the kitchen window.

"Every day," I answered, remembering how happy we were while we were there, and how much I enjoyed the farm.

"I want to raise Dakota the way Jacob and Katie raise their kids, away from hate, drugs, and crime," she said.

"There's nothing holding us here, Bobby. Why don't we move to Missouri and live with the Amish?"

I told her about my conversation with Jacob, explaining that as head of the house, in the Amish tradition, I would need an Amish sponsor and the bishop's approval. I then told her Jacob had offered to sponsor me.

"So, can we move there?" she asked, looking at me through the eyes of a little girl asking for her first bicycle.

"Are you sure this is what you want?" I asked.

"I'm sure," she said.

Tanner called that evening, asking if he could bring a friend over for dinner. Shelly said yes, and asked him to pick up a gallon of milk on his way.

"We've missed you. Where've you been hanging out?" Shelly asked as Tanner and his friend sat down at the table for dinner.

"I've been staying at Jerry's. We go to the lake every day, lay out in the sun and pick up chicks. Have you heard from Jacob?" Tanner asked.

"No. Why?" Shelly questioned, looking at Tanner, then back at me.

"Oh, I just thought he might call or somethin'," Tanner replied, appearing discouraged.

"Is that the Amish man you were telling me about?" Tanner's friend asked, "The one with the pretty daughter?"

"Yes, Mandy," Tanner answered, grinning shyly.

"Tanner said she taught him some German words. She sounds pretty cool."

"Oh, really?" Shelly asked, winking at me.

"I guess you'll miss us then, when we move to Missouri, won't ya," Shelly said, smiling demurely, passing a bowl of gravy to Tanner, holding it firmly in her hand as he tried to take it from her.

"What! Are you serious? You're moving to Missouri?" Tanner shouted, tugging at the bowl.

"Yes, can you believe it?" Shelly screamed.

"Oh, my God! I can't wait to tell my friends! I want to come! I'll go to college later!" Tanner cried out.

We stayed up most of the night, excited about our decision and making plans for our move. I called Jacob's English neighbor the next day and left a message for Jacob to return my call. Jacob called early the next evening. I told him the news and asked if he would look for a house for us to rent. He said there was an old empty farm house down the road a piece from his place that was owned by a good friend of the

Amish, and that he would contact him right away to see if it was available, and livable.

Jacob called me three days later and said the farm house was available, needed some fixing up, and if I was willing to do some minor repairs on it I could rent it for $50.00 a month.

I told him we'd take it.

It was a beautiful, warm sunny day as I turned on the dirt road to the Missouri farmhouse. Alongside the borrow-pit, nestled in native grasses, yellow, gold, and orange wildflowers soaked up the warmth of the sun. Nearing the farm house, I realized that this was the first step of our life with the Amish.

Checking the mailbox numbers, I pulled our car into the driveway, turned off the ignition, took a deep breath, and exhaled. I was happy to be alive, happy to be on the farm, and excited about what our future had in store for us.

Peering through the windshield, I saw a clapboard plank farm house with an asphalt shingle roof and a large porch. The tired and beaten old building stood in a fenced yard, behind a broad-branched, gnarled cottonwood tree. The front door screen, missing a hinge, hung precariously from its door frame. Rotted steps lay in a heap on the ground at the base of the front porch. A wasp nest hung by a strand above an open window. Broken glass from a second floor window lay scattered on the ground.

Ambling slowly toward us from the back of the house was a large, flop-eared cur dog, looking as if he hadn't eaten in a week. (Dakota later named him Biscuit for his uncanny ability to snatch the hot, buttered morsels from Shelly's hand.) I opened the car door, stepped out on the ground, stretched my arms toward the sky and said, "We're home!"

Leaning the dilapidated screen door back against the house, I opened the large wood frame door and walked into the front room. Layers of tattered and torn wall paper hung from the walls as reminders of better days. A wood stove stood solitarily against the east wall. A large kitchen sat to the left. Straight ahead was a stairwell leading to the upstairs bedrooms.

Looking through the house, sizing up what needed to be done, I walked outside and into the barn where my nostrils were greeted by the pungent smell of urine and rotted hay. Flies, swarming over decomposed manure, scattered as I walked past them.

The barn had six stalls, three on either side with a rickety ladder leading to the hay loft. I dropped to my knees as barn swallows flew toward me from the safety of the loft, the thrust from their wings mussing my hair. Standing up, I heard the loud and distinct croaking sounds of bullfrogs and walked outside to see a large, murky pond under a massive elm tree located between the farm house and several acres of fenced pasture.

Butterflies fluttered lightly past my head, then darted around me, lighting on tall, green, blade-like spears growing around the banks of the pond. Wild honey bees and bumble bees danced from blossom to blossom. Colorful birds sang their beautiful songs as they took flight through the willows. Sitting on the grass, I relaxed, stretched out my body and listened to the sounds of the country. I breathed in the sweet smell and the taste of unpolluted air, allowing my mind to wander; dismissing my fears, anxiety, and thoughts of the challenges that lay ahead. God had brought us here to heal, to make a new life for ourselves. This was my belief, and what I trusted in Him to show me.

Returning to the house, I found Shelly cleaning kitchen cabinets and drawers.

"We have a lot of work to do!" she said, opening a wooden drawer, blowing particles of fine dust away from her face, causing her to sneeze.

Tanner and I spent the next week cleaning, moving furniture and making repairs in and around the house. I decided to paint the downstairs walls and found a note on the kitchen counter saying there was paint in the front room closet. Opening the closet door, I found a five gallon bucket of paint, a variety of well-used brushes and a tray and a stir stick, apparently left by the home owner.

Using my Buck knife I removed the top from the bucket, stirred the paint, poured a good amount in the tray, walked across the room, turned on my stereo and placed a vinyl album on the record player.

I'm going to make this old house come alive, I thought to myself, dipping the brush into the white paint.

I'd no sooner begun painting when I heard a loud knock on the front door. Setting my paint brush back in the tray I opened the door and was greeted by Jacob and Katie.

"Come in and have a cup of coffee with us!" I said, happy they'd stopped to see us.

Declining, they said they were just passing by and stopped because they thought they'd heard music coming from the farm house.

Excusing myself, I walked over to the stereo, raised the arm from the album and suddenly remembered I was told not to use the electricity.

"What was that tune?" Katie asked, before I could utter a word in my defense.

"*Amazing Grace,* my favorite inspirational song," I replied, hoping some semblance of leniency might be forthcoming.

Katie turned to Jacob and spoke softly in German. He nodded.

"Would you mind playing it for me?" she asked politely.

Stunned, I looked questioningly at Shelly, back at Katie, and placed the needle on the album.

Thanking me as the song ended, Katie clasped her hands together, placed them against her body and moved close to Jacob.

Clearing his throat, Jacob looked directly into my eyes, squared his shoulders, and reminded me that I was not to use the house electricity, and furthermore, that I would need to sell my stereo, or give it to someone if I had intentions of living in the Amish community. I told him I was sorry if I had offended them and would get rid of it as quickly as possible.

Bidding us good-bye, Jacob and Katie climbed in their buggy and clattered away. I had learned a hard lesson, one of many to come, one that reminded me of the many sacrifices the Amish make every day of their lives.

Tanner and I worked until after midnight that evening, painting rooms and performing minor repairs. Using pump water and double-basin wash tubs, Shelly cleaned the kitchen and scrubbed the floors. Feeling summarily reprimanded, we entertained ourselves whistling, singing our favorite tunes, and laughing about what our friends and relatives would say if they heard about what had happened to us that day.

After weeks of working to make the farm house livable I decided it was time to talk to Jacob about becoming part of the Amish community. Walking to his farm one brisk morning I found him in his barn and asked when might be a good time to visit the church bishop. He said he'd spoken with the bishop and would speak to him again now that we were settled.

The next day, as I was cleaning the stalls, the owner of the farm stopped by and introduced himself. A large, imposing man in his early fifties with soft eyes, thick square shoulders, massive hands and a Midwestern accent, he introduced himself as Charlie Johnson.

Complimenting me on the repairs we'd made to the house, yard and barn, he said he was happy to have us living on the old place.

I'd parked my car in the barn and planned to advertise it in the local paper when I had the time. Seeing it, Charlie asked if it was for sale. I told him I had no need for it that it was in good condition and asked if he knew anyone who might be interested in buying it.

"Guess you'll be needin' money soon to buy a horse and buggy won't ya!" he said, slapping me hard on my back, laughing out loud.

He said his son needed a dependable work car, took a look under the hood, at the interior and kicked the tires. We haggled over the price until he realized I wasn't going to budge. Pulling a wallet from his back pocket, he counted out the cash in twenties and placed them in my hand, smiling as he took out the first month's rent.

"Wait, I have something for your son," I said, remembering my conversation with Jacob. Stepping into the house, I loaded my stereo system in a large cardboard box, carried it outside, and handed it to him.

"I heard about your run-in with Jacob!" he said. "Those Amish folks are pretty particular about not using electricity. I'd watch myself! They're keepin' a close eye on you!"

The following Sunday, Jacob and Katie stopped by on their way home from church. Petie, Joseph, Jonas and Barbara came in the house. Mandy, Andy, and Mattie stayed outside to visit with Tanner and Dakota.

Katie commented on how nice the house looked, asked Shelly if she'd like to come over and learn how to sew on her treadle machine, and said Mandy had some clothes she could wear until she made some for herself. She said Shelly could use her machine and some of her material to make Tanner, Dakota and me some clothes.

Walking outside, Jacob and I strolled to the barn and discussed what farm animals I would need. He said I should have a few laying hens, a sow with piglets, and a good milk cow.

"Once you begin growing your own garden and canning your own food, you'll be self-sufficient. We'll bring some canned food over soon to get you'ns started and we'll go to the auction next Tuesday to buy your farm animals. I have a gentle mare you can use until you can afford to buy a buggy horse of your own.

My brother Levi has a buggy and harness shop and always has a few good used ones for sale. We'll stop by his farm on the way home from the auction and see what he has in stock," he said, throwing a stick into the pond, watching its wake reach the water's edge.

"By the way," he said, lighting his pipe, "I spoke with the bishop. He wants to see us Thursday afternoon."

We returned to the house, sat down at the kitchen table, drank a cup of coffee, and talked about repair projects he wanted me to help him with on his farm.

"See ya early Tuesday morning!" he shouted, pulling out on the dirt road, snapping the reins, disappearing in a cloud of dust.

Tuesday morning arrived. Jacob pulled up to the farm house with Mandy sitting on the front seat next to him. His roan gelding snorted and pawed nervously at the ground as Jacob stepped down from the buggy and walked up the stairs to the porch.

"Katie was wonderin' if you might wanna come over to the house and sew some today," Jacob said, stepping into the house.

"I'd love to!" Shelly said, grabbing her jacket, throwing it over her shoulders and walking outside. Tanner was standing next to the buggy, holding Dakota's hand and visiting with Mandy.

The morning air was chilly and the topless, three-seated buggy provided little protection against the elements. Jacob sat on the hardwood bench seat, snapped the reins, shouted a command and turned the buggy westward toward his farm.

Clinging to each other, laughing loudly as the buggy bolted forward, Shelly and I felt like children on a Disneyland ride. Mandy turned, looked at us, and smiled politely as we sped away, as if she understood the excitement and joy we were experiencing riding in a horse drawn buggy for the first time.

Pulling our jackets tightly against our bodies we snuggled close together, bracing ourselves as we raced down the bumpy dirt road. I'll never forget the sweet smell of Jacob's horse, the feeling of the wind against my face, and the sound of the wooden spoke wheels as we dashed across the Missouri countryside that morning.

Driving past fenced pastures, watching as small flocks of birds flew from post to post, I couldn't help but wonder what questions the bishop would ask me on Thursday, and what we would do if he refused to allow us to live in the settlement and attend Amish church services?

We dropped off Mandy and Shelly and left for the auction.

The fifteen-mile ride to the auction took us off the dirt road and onto a two-lane paved state highway. A car sped by, honking loudly as it passed and turned quickly back in front of the buggy. I thought of the picture I'd seen of the overturned buggy in the newspaper back in Oklahoma City only a short while ago, although now, sitting next to Jacob in a horse drawn buggy, it seemed as if it were a lifetime ago.

Jacob snapped the reins sharply, barked a command and brought the gelding to a brisk trot.

5

The Auction

The gravel auction parking lot was filled with Amish buggies, and cars and trucks of all sizes. Jacob parked among the other Amish buggies and walked past a group of English farmers dressed in bib overalls, short-sleeve shirts, straw hats and rubber boots. Sipping coffee and smoking cigarettes, they cursed loudly, talking about the weather and the cost of farming.

Huddled together in a group a few yards away were thirty or more Amish men, joking with each other, telling stories and enjoying each other's company.

Stopping to greet them, Jacob introduced me.

"So, this is the Englishmen we've heard so much about," stated one of the elders.

"How do ya like livin' in the old Johnson farmhouse?"

"It was pretty rough at first," I replied, "but we've made a lot of improvements, and like it just fine now," feeling a sense of pride.

"We would've been happy to help out, ya know," commented another.

"Thank you. I appreciate that."

"What are you lookin' to buy?"

"Jacob's helping me pick out a good sow, chickens, and a milk cow."

"Well, you're in good hands. Good luck to ya! Hope to see you in church soon!"

"We'd better get inside," Jacob said.

"Nice to meet you," I said, walking away.

As much as I enjoyed being at the auction, and appreciated the offer of help from the Amish elders, I felt like a fish out of water.

Was I an Englishmen? Was I Amish? It was as though I had lost any identity I may have had and didn't belong with either. Was I getting myself into something I couldn't handle? Had I gotten in over my head?

I followed Jacob inside the building, sat down, and waited for the auction to begin.

The auctioneer turned on the microphone and called for the first cow. A low, deep buzz filled the building. Jacob told me an Amish cousin had brought a fresh Jersey to sell, and that we would wait for her number to be called. Grandpa Bolin had Jersey cows on his farm, and told me that he preferred them over the other breeds because they were easy to maintain and gave rich, creamy milk. I felt close to him, knowing I might take one home.

A few Jerseys and Holsteins passed through the ring when Jacob tugged on my shirt sleeve and said, "There she is Bob. That's the one. She's a real beaut!" He pointed eagerly at the heifer being led into the ring. I removed my bid card from my shirt pocket, placed it on my lap, and sat up straight.

After considerable haggling I bought my first farm animal that morning. I hoped it would be one of several to come. Having taken the first step, I was somewhat relieved and feeling confident.

I wondered what the bishop would say, now that I had made this commitment.

"I know this breeder," Jacob said, stopping in front of a pen in the swine building.

We'd left the arena and were looking for a good sow with pigs.

"Morning, Jacob!" a friendly voice called out from behind.

"Hello, Tom," Jacob said, turning, shaking the man's hand.

"Who's your friend?" Tom asked, looking at me with a sense of keen interest.

Jacob introduced me, said my family and I were new to the area, that we hoped to join the Amish church soon, and that I needed a good sow, piglets and some chickens.

"Well, if you're interested in my sow and piglets, I'll sell em' to you at a fair price, and I'll throw in some good layers to boot! How does that sound?"

Jacob told Tom I'd bought a cow and that I was looking for a way to get her home.

Tom laughed and said, "Tell ya what, Bob. Any friend of Jacob's is a friend of mine. You seem like a nice feller. I'll deliver the whole kit-and-caboodle tomorrow! Do we have a deal?"

"I guess so," I said, looking to Jacob for support.

"You've got a deal!" Jacob said, shaking Tom's hand.

I settled with the auctioneer and we were on our way.

"How'd I do? I've never bought anything at an auction, "I queried Jacob, passing an Amish buggy on the highway.

"You did fine, Bob, just fine," Jacob replied, shifting the reins to his left hand, tapping me on my back with his right hand.

Jacob turned his buggy off the highway and onto the long drive leading to Levi's farm house. A handsome man in his early forties with a raven black beard, black eyes and thick curly black hair that cupped up under his hat and over his ears, Levi walked out of his shop to meet us.

I watched as he grew near. His shirtsleeves were rolled up, revealing dark, muscular forearms and hands. His wide shoulders formed a natural "V" as they cut to his small waist. He appeared to be good-humored, a man who enjoyed life and made friends easily, but it was also evident that he was a man of strong resolve.

I liked him immediately.

"What can I do for you?" he asked.

Jacob introduced us and said, "Bob needs a good buggy and harness."

"I have a buggy I've done some repair work on that'll be ready early next week, and I could sell you that harness hanging over there in the corner of the shop. They're both in pretty good shape."

Inspecting the buggy, then the harness, Jacob inquired, "What's your best price for the both of them?"

"Two hundred and fifty dollars. You won't find a better deal anywhere!"

"We'll pick em' up next week!" Jacob said, giving me a nod, a wink, and a knowing glance.

"What are you gonna' pull that buggy with?" Levi asked. "Ya know, Eli's got a freshly trained thoroughbred gelding for sale."

"Eli's gelding is much too young and too high-spirited for Bob and his family. I'm gonna let him use Maggie for a while."

"Oh! Yeah! Ol' Maggie! She's a dandy, and will suit him and his family just fine! How old is Maggie now?"

"She'll be fifteen this fall, but she still has some life left in her!" Jacob said, laughing heartily.

Levi said he'd heard we were living on Charlie Johnson's place and asked if I'd met Eli. I told him I had not.

"Eli trains buggy horses. He's also an excellent carpenter and cabinet builder. He's always lookin' for help. Are you lookin' for work?"

I told him I would be soon.

"I'll see him at church Sunday and tell him I talked to you."

"Thank you," I said, shaking his hand.

"We'll see you next week," Jacob shouted, as we pulled out onto the highway and trotted away.

The buggy ride to Jacob's farm went quickly. The sun had warmed the earth. White clouds, looking like soft cotton balls, hung from the satiny blue sky. The sound of bees humming and birds singing filled the still air. A light cloud of dust followed closely behind the buggy as we turned onto the dirt road.

Pulling up to the farm house, I realized, "Soon, I'll be driving my own buggy and taking my family to church on Sundays."

"Hurry! Hurry! I want to show you something!" Shelly shouted almost frantically, running out of the house, her eyes filled with anticipation.

"What is it?" I asked, leaping from the buggy, wondering what might be the matter.

"Come look!"

Following her up the stairs, into the house, and across the room I saw a black dress hanging loosely over the back of a rocking chair.

On the seat, lying across the worn arms was a gray apron and a black bonnet.

"Isn't it pretty?" she asked, picking up the dress, holding it against her slim body.

"It's beautiful! Who made it?" I questioned, certain as to the answer of my question.

"I did!" She exclaimed.

Jacob walked through the front door, brushed himself off, removed his hat and held it in his hand. Seeing the clothing Shelly had made, and how excited she was, he looked at Katie, standing in the kitchen doorway and winked. Returning his wink, she looked back at Shelly.

"She did a good job, didn't she?" Katie said, looking at Jacob, then at me.

"A fine job!" Jacob said.

"Why don't you put it on for all to see?" Katie said, looking down the hallway toward the bedroom.

"Can I? I mean, could I? Are you sure that would be okay? " Shelly asked, removing the dress from the rocker.

"Why yes! Now hurry along to the bedroom and put it on. Bob wants to see what it looks like on you!"

"I'll be right back!" she replied, quickly leaving the room.

"She's learning to sew very quickly," Katie said, walking into the front room, sitting down on a wooden chair.

"I'll get us some coffee," Jacob said, strolling to the kitchen.

A few minutes passed, the bedroom door opened, and Shelly walked into the front room.

"It fits perfectly!" Katie exclaimed, rising from her chair.

I'd never seen Shelly look so radiant, so happy. Tears of joy welled up in her eyes as she stood next to me and placed her trembling hand in mine.

"Do you like it?" she asked, whispering in my ear.

"I love it." I said softly, pulling her close to me. "You look very pretty."

Jacob and Katie, attempting to provide privacy to this special moment, disappeared into the kitchen.

"Well then, let's have some coffee and cookies!" Jacob called out.

"I understand Jacob's taking you to see the bishop on Thursday," Katie remarked.

"Yes, and I'm very nervous," I replied, taking a bite of cookie and a sip of coffee.

"Everything works according to God's plan," she replied. "If this is meant to be, it will happen."

"What if he says no?" Shelly asked nervously.

"Now! Now! Don't you give that another thought! You came here for a reason. We must trust and believe in God that this was meant to be. You will pray, and you will have faith about this. Now you just put those thoughts right out of your mind!"

Silence filled the room. We finished our coffee and cookies.

What would we do if the bishop said no? I wondered. *Would we return to Oklahoma? Would we go back to California? Where would we find the money to replace everything we'd sold? Would our marriage make it through this crisis?*

The thought of it made me break into a cold sweat.

Shelly reached under the table, squeezed my hand, and looked at me through concerned eyes.

"Would you like another cookie?" Katie asked, passing the plate around the table.

"Thank you. I think we'd better get goin' now," I said, rising from my chair.

"I'll get the buggy," Jacob said, grabbing his hat, stepping outside.

Tom delivered the cow, pigs, and chickens the following Wednesday morning, along with several bales of hay and a sack of corn.

"Let me know when you need more," he said, shaking my hand.

"Thank you so much for all the help you've been."

"My pleasure," he said, turning and climbing back in his truck.

Thursday afternoon came quickly. I knew Jacob was on his way to pick me up for our meeting with the bishop. The uncertainty was stifling. I heard a buggy pull up and looked out the window to see him holding the reins in his hand and looking toward the house.

"Are you ready?" he shouted toward the house.

"I'll be right there!"

My heart was pounding. Beads of perspiration were forming on my forehead.

"I'm going now. Pray for me…" I said, holding Shelly close to me.

"You'll do fine," she said, softly. "Just remember Katie's words."

6

Dream Becomes Reality

The Amish have rejected coercive powers as worldly, priding themselves instead on humility, simplicity, and obedience. The selection of a person to lead their membership is an important process. Forwardness and any idiosyncrasies are frowned upon, while being a solid manager of his family and farm are highly regarded and respected.

Preparing himself to become a bishop is not something an Amish man would do, no more than he would announce he had been called by God, or attend a seminary. These things, in the eyes of the Amish, are sure signs of a loss of humility, and the development of an ego.

The self-governing unit of the Amish is the church, while the bishop is the leader of the church and its head authority. He administers rites of communication, baptism, marriage, excommunication, and sometimes allows "backsliders" to be reinstated into the church.

One of the bishop's numerous duties is to maintain his settlement so that its 25-40 families can meet in a single household on church Sundays. He is assisted by two preachers who are expected to preach when he appoints them to do so.

Each Amish church member has been taught to be "unspotted from the world," and to keep separate from the usual human desires and goals. Baptism into the Amish church requires members to be adults and to choose for him or herself. If a young person chooses to leave the Amish faith, this is the time they typically act upon that decision.

Jacob and I pulled into the bishop's drive and tied off the roan gelding. Knocking gently on the door, Jacob took a step back and waited. The bishop opened the door, asked us to please come in and offered us a cup of coffee.

Like many Amish men, the bishop was a farmer. Small in stature, his movement was graceful and projected a sense of serenity and self-confidence.

"You have come to seek membership in the Amish church. Is this correct?" he asked.

"Yes sir, I have."

"Can you tell me what thought process or events in your life brought you to this decision?"

"My Grandpa Bolin is a church pastor. I love him dearly and hold him in the highest regard. He taught me as a young boy about the virtues of hard work, sacrifice, family values, respecting others, of being a God-fearing man and to live a life that would make my family proud. It was grandpa's teaching's that led me to the simple life and spiritual ways of the Amish. I've tried to follow his teachings, but have failed. I want the Amish way of life for myself, and for my family."

The bishop spoke. "We are a plain people. We do not seek material things, and refrain from that which is of this world. We believe the world will soon collapse, and that he who lives the will of God will move into a new age. We believe that Salvation is to be found in the community of those who withdraw from involvement in the affairs of mankind. It is not our way, nor our desire, to become like the English. Instead, we choose to place a screen between ourselves and the outside world, thereby limiting the flow of information coming into our communities. We honor our fathers and our mothers and teach our children at an early age to work and show respect for their elders. We separate ourselves by our outward appearance and the clothes we wear. We do not seek self-gratification or, to bring attention to ourselves. We shun modern comforts and self-enhancement. We help each other in time of need. Has Jacob explained the importance of these things to you?"

I told him I'd learned much about the Amish from Jacob that I'd shared these things with my family, of how eager we were to become members of the community, and to begin attending church services.

"I have spoken with Jacob and am confident of your desire to join the Amish community. Please step outside. Jacob will join you there shortly."

I paced back and forth in front of the house, then the yard, and finally the long drive. Did I say the right things? What did he think of me?

Five, ten, twenty minutes went by. The front door opened. Jacob stepped outside, his eyes facing down, revealing only the top of his black felt hat. Walking slowly toward me, he raised his head and extended his hand toward mine.

"The bishop has approved your request. You are now a member of the Amish community!"

I was so excited I wanted to hug him. Hug the bishop. Hug his wife. Run as fast as I could all the way home and tell Shelly the good news. The worry and anxiety of the past few weeks vanished into thin air. The weight that'd been lying heavily on my shoulders was gone.

I stopped, said a silent prayer, and thanked God for his love and mercy.

The trip home seemed like an eternity. Jacob stopped his buggy at our farm. I thanked him for standing by me. He shook my hand, turned his buggy and left for home, looking pleased and satisfied.

Tanner peered out the door and called out loudly saying, "What happened, Bobby?"

"The bishop approved my request!" I shouted back at the top of my voice, my heart filled with joy.

"Does that mean we can stay?" he yelled back, standing on the porch, smiling from ear to ear.

I walked up the pathway to the porch, took a deep breath, exhaled, and shouted as loudly as I could, "Yes, we can stay!"

Shelly ran from the kitchen, opened the front door, and stepped outside on the porch. Grabbing me by the shoulders, she looked into my eyes and said: "Is this true, Bobby? You're not lying?"

"Can you bear to hear what happened?" I asked, returning her look.

"I can bear anything, except not knowing what happened today." Tell me, tell me *now*," she said, laying the palest shadow of stress upon the last word.

"The bishop said I could become a member of the community," I replied, taking her in my arms, holding her close to me.

"Oh, Bobby, I'm so happy. I didn't know what we were going to do if he had said no," she answered, bursting into tears, pressing her face against my chest.

"What about Tanner, Dakota, and me?" she asked. "What will happen to us?"

"Jacob says Tanner will have to talk to the bishop about joining the church on his own. There's no hurry for you, and Dakota won't be able to become a church member until he is in his late teens."

The following Monday morning Tanner and I walked to Jacob's farm to pick up Maggie. A small, fine-boned, sorrel mare, with a white blaze on her forehead and four white socks, Maggie's fire, if she ever did indeed possess any, had long since been extinguished. She was slow, deliberate, and steady as a fined-tuned clock.

She was exactly what I needed…

"So, you came to pick up Maggie!" Jacob said, approaching us as we walked toward the barn.

"Yep! Is she ready?"

"She sure is. Petie fed and curried her this morning. I reckon she's as ready as she'll ever be. Do you need some help getting her back to your farm?"

"No thanks. We can make it, I'm sure."

"She's there in the stall. Let me know if you have any problems with her!" Jacob said, walking to the porch, sitting down in a rocker, lighting his pipe.

I entered the barn, opened the stall door, hooked a lead rope around Maggie's neck and led her outside.

"I'm gonna' stick around here awhile," Tanner said, looking at me coyly, standing next to Mandy outside the barn.

"Okay. I'll see you back at the farm. Don't be late for dinner! You know how your sister is!"

Tanner had always had his way with English women. I wondered if Mandy would fall under his spell as quickly as the others had.

I walked Maggie home, allowing her to stop and graze on the tall Johnson grass growing out of the borrow pit along the way. It was a clear, bright beautiful sunny day. A gentle westward breeze blew at my back. A bluebird sang his song as he followed us along the dusty lane. Landing on a post, he sat perfectly still, as if posing for a portrait.

I was eager to hook Maggie up to my buggy and take her out for our first outing, but was in no hurry. It was a fine day to be alive. Arriving home, I put her in a stall, threw her a block of hay and took a closer look at her.

"Where's Tanner?" Shelly asked, walking up behind me.

"He stayed behind to visit with Mandy."

"I think he likes her," Shelly answered, with a concerned look on her face. "She's not like English girls. He won't have his way with her."

"I think she'll handle him just fine. You needn't worry," I replied.

"I hope you're right. I'd hate for him to get us, *or her,* in trouble."

"It'll be okay. Let's go in the house and have a bite to eat."

Just then, Dakota began chasing Shelly with a large slimy frog he'd caught in the pond, laughing loudly as she ran ahead of him.

"Get away from me, Dakota!" She screamed, jumping up and down, running into the front room. "Bobby, make him stop!" she cried out loud, now laughing frantically.

Enjoying the farm and all the critters on the property, we had to check his pockets every night for frogs, grasshoppers, and other creatures he'd found while playing outside.

The next morning, as I was finishing a bowl of mush, some hot buttered biscuits, and a glass of fresh warm milk, I heard a buggy pull up the drive. Shoveling the remaining mush down, I drank my milk and asked Shelly to save a biscuit for me.

Jacob stepped down from the buggy and tethered his horse.

"C'mon in," I said, opening the door.

"Katie sent you'ns some canned vegetables, meat, and fruit," he said, helping Petie lift a large box out of the back of the buggy. Jacob carried the box in the house and sat down at the kitchen table. Petie carried five more boxes in and sat them on the kitchen floor.

"Thank you, Jacob. Please tell Katie how much we appreciate this," Shelly said softly, reaching out to shake his hand.

"No need to thank us. We help each other. It is our way. One day you'll be asked to do the same for others in our community."

7

A New Buggy and a Ride to Remember

I heard a commotion outside and opened the door to see Levi and Jacob pulling up in Jacob's buggy. They were being followed by another buggy, pulled by a beautiful black Standardbred stud, driven by an Amish man I did not recognize. I walked outside and quickly realized the second buggy was the one I'd purchased from Levi. Jacob stepped down, told me they'd decided to deliver my buggy, and introduced me to Eli.

Eli was a striking man in his early twenties. His thick black hair and beard framed a sharp nose, tight mouth and keen, hawk-like eyes that seemed to look straight into my soul.

His shoulders were rounded and muscular, and his bulging forearms were coupled with small, compact hands.

Jacob said Eli would ride back with them, and return later to provide me with a few pointers on how to hook up Maggie to the harness and drive her. We visited a few minutes as Eli unharnessed his thoroughbred and tied him to the back of Jacob's buggy. I paid Levi the money I owed him and they left.

A few hours passed when I heard a buggy coming at breakneck speed down the dirt lane. Peering over my shoulder from the stall where I was standing, I watched as the buggy slowed and pulled into our farm.

I instantly recognized the stud, and observed Eli as he climbed out of his buggy and jumped to the ground. Spinning around slowly he patted the stud's moist neck.

"Guten Tag!" he shouted, walking toward me.

"Hello!"

"So tell me Bob what experience you have working with horses," he said, reaching out to shake my hand.

I remembered something Grandpa had told me many years before.

"Always shake a feller's hand with a good, firm grip. A limp hand shake is a sure sign of a weak man."

Placing my hand in Eli's, I felt as though my fingers were being crushed as he tightened his grip. It was as though I had placed my hand in a vice and the jaws were slowly crushing the life out of my fingers.

"I have some experience riding horses," I said, retracting my hand, feeling the blood rushing life back into it.

Eli said the Amish do not ride horses. "Horses were placed here by God to be used for labor, not for pleasure," he said smugly.

I had visions of a runaway horse, galloping at full speed down the highway and me, standing on the seat, pulling hard on the reins screaming, "Whoa! Stop!" Little did I know at the time about the accuracy of this premonition.

Eli took the harness off his stud, led him to my buggy and began harnessing him, explaining each move he'd made. Asking me to remove the harness and put it back on, we went through the process several times until I felt comfortable doing it alone. Harnessing the stud for the last time, Eli said it was time for a drive.

I climbed into the buggy next to Eli and had no sooner sat down when he snapped the reins and shouted a command. Bolting as if he'd seen a ghost, the stud leapt forward, hitting full stride in a matter of seconds.

My feet flew up in the air. My elbows landed hard against the floorboard. Speeding down the dirt lane as if we were on a collision course with the devil himself, it took all the strength I had to pull myself upright again. The thrust of the start and speed of the buggy were enthralling. I felt like I was on a race track at Hialeah, coming down the backstretch, speeding toward the finish line. Eli looked over at me as I righted myself and smiled.

Fence posts became a blur. The stud raised his head and neck up high in the air as he trotted at full speed. His long, flowing mane flew through the air as if weightless. His breathing was quick, loud and deep. The muscles in his back, neck and legs extended, then gathered in knots as his long body maintained the frantic pace. The sound of his hooves pounding on the dirt road was deafening. Lather began forming on his neck and massive quarters.

I'd never been as excited, and fearful, as I was that day, and have not been since.

Eli began pulling back on the reins as we neared the end of the road. I watched as he turned the buggy around and pointed it in the direction of home. "I can do that," I thought, as we headed back to the farm.

Another hard lesson was about to be learned...

Returning home, I unharnessed the stud, wiped him down, put him in a stall and hitched Maggie to my buggy. Eli climbed on the passenger side of the seat, reached over, took the reins in his hand and asked if I was ready.

I told him I was as ready as I ever would be and stepped up to the seat. He told me to get settled in my seat, snap the reins smartly and shout, "*Schnell*!" when I was ready. Arranging the reins in my hand as Eli had done, I took a deep breath and said softly, "Giddy-up!"

Maggie pawed the ground, snorted loudly, turned her head, and looked at me. I felt like an idiot. Frustrated that she hadn't budged, Eli said I had to let Maggie know who was boss. He told me to snap the reins hard against her rump and shout the command as though I meant it. I was afraid she would bolt, and leave me sitting in the back seat if I shouted, "*Schnell,*" but was concerned that if I didn't, I would offend Eli.

Gripping the reins tightly in my hands, I snapped them sharply and shouted, "*Schnell!*" as loudly, and with as much authority, as I could muster. True to her nature, Maggie took a step forward, and broke into a slow, even trot.

Listening closely to Eli's instructions, I practiced pulling on the reins, turning slightly to the right, then to the left, as we drove down the road. Maggie took it all in stride, ostensibly anticipating my expectations of her.

We came to the end of the lane and I yelled, "Whoa!" Maggie stopped. Remembering how Eli turned the buggy around with apparent ease, I pulled back on both reins. Maggie stood still. I pulled harder.

Nothing...

With the reins still in my hands, Eli reached over, pulled on the right rein and shouted, *"Zuruck!* [Back!]" Maggie backed hard to the right and stopped. He then pulled hard on the left rein. Maggie stepped forward and to the left. Eli let go of the reins and told me to straighten out the buggy. Before I could utter a command, Maggie turned, and with a reluctant start, trotted slowly back toward home.

"You did well," Eli said, stepping down from the buggy. Embarrassed, and still smarting from appearing so green, I unharnessed Maggie, put her away, and gave her a bucket of oats. Eli led the stud out of the stall and hooked him to his buggy.

"I have some work for you if you're interested," he said, stepping into his buggy. "Enough to keep you and Tanner busy all summer if you like."

I thanked him, told him we could use the money, and asked him to let me know when we would begin.

Every task the Amish perform has an order and a methodology to it. Nothing is left to chance. Friday is housekeeping day. Saturday is reserved for yard work. Sundays are spent in church, or visiting other Amish families. Monday is wash day.

We were now wearing Amish clothing, thanks to contributions from several Amish families and Shelly learning how to sew. My beard was beginning to look somewhat full. Shelly looked angelic in her black dress, apron and bonnet.

Dakota loved the sound his suspenders made when he snapped them against his barrel chest. Amish boys wear dresses until they are two years of age, at which time they are replaced with trousers, a shirt and a stiff black, broad-brimmed hat. He'd accepted the change from the English world to the Amish ways without much ado. He spent most of his time chasing butterflies, playing with Biscuit, and asking questions only a three year old boy could ask.

Tanner wore clothing donated by several Amish families. He'd been told by Jacob he could wear Amish clothing as long as he behaved in a manner representative of the Amish lifestyle and values.

Working with a crew constructing a small store in a town twenty miles away, he spent most of his leisure time with Mandy. I worked with Eli building and installing kitchen cabinets in English homes. It was common knowledge that he was the finest cabinet maker in the county, be it English, or Amish.

The hens were laying, the pigs would be ready for slaughter after the first frost. Life on the farm was good.

8

Rural Life

The Amish are meticulous farmers. Believing that with practical knowledge and hard work a living can be made from the soil, they feel the farm is the rightful place for their families.

They refuse to accept direct cash subsidies from the government, believe receiving "artificial income" would introduce dangers, and that the moral consequences of accepting government aid would erode their conscience and their motivation. Having realized an agreeable level, they choose not to live on a higher standard than they are comfortable with.

"Trying to live above our means would be prideful and arrogant. We will not succumb to this manner of thinking," one Amish farmer told me.

While they buy staple foods such as sugar, flour, and salt at the market, the Amish have retained nineteenth century customs and technologies to plant and harvest their crops. This is as sacred to them as singing and praying. Each farm produces hundreds of quarts of meat, vegetables, and fruit each year.

When asked why they don't use tractors to plow their fields, another Amish farmer stated, "Tractors don't make manure. They ruin the land."

Gardening was new to Shelly and me. While our parents grew up on farms and had gardens, we had no experience cultivating, planting, or harvesting vegetables. Desiring to have a productive garden as other Amish women did, Shelly helped Katie and Mandy prepare and plant theirs, learning the proper techniques of digging rows, planting seeds and watering. We tilled and seeded the ground for our garden, carefully following Katie's instructions about how far apart, how deep, how much fertilizer, and how much water to use.

Planting corn, tomatoes, green beans, and potatoes our first year, we watched anxiously as the ground began to separate and small, green wrinkled sprouts began to appear on the surface of the soil.

Excited and proud about the beginning of our first garden together, Shelly jumped in the buggy, raced down the dirt lane to Jacob and Katie's farm with her bonnet half-tied, waving in the wind, and invited Jacob, Katie and Mandy to come and see what she called, "our miracle garden."

The fruits of our labor began to grace our table as the summer progressed.

Later in the year, Shelly, Katie, and Mandy spent weeks canning tomatoes and other vegetables from the garden. Shelly and Dakota sat on the front porch in the cool of the evening, snapping beans, peeling potatoes and waving as members of the Amish community passed by in their buggies—shouting *"Guten Tag*! *Wie geht es dir?"*

Dakota, taking to the farm life quickly, got out of bed early every morning to help Shelly water the garden, gather eggs, throw corn to the chickens and feed the pigs. After breakfast, he ran out of the house into the backyard and jumped on the swing I had hung on a high, strong limb of an old hickory tree.

I asked Petie to come over one morning and show me the proper technique of milking a cow. He'd been milking her for us and I figured it was time for me to learn. Assessing the situation as I looked at Goldie's udder, I figured it was pretty straightforward.

You pull on the teat and warm, white, sweet milk comes out. How difficult could that be?

Another lesson was about to be learned...

Walking Goldie in from the pasture, I tied her off in the stall and backed away. Petie took the stool he'd brought with him and told me to set it close to Goldie's hindquarters. Placing the stool and bucket next to her udder, I sat down, dipped my hand into the cold sudsy water we'd mixed and brought a handful up to her warm udder. The next thing I remember is finding myself sprawled across the dirt floor, lying flat on my back, my face red, my pride bruised.

Apparently unhappy with the manner in which I approached her udder, Goldie proceeded to kicked me off the milk stool. Mooing loudly, she swished her tail back and forth, and continued chewing her cud. Petie, trying unsuccessfully to control his laughter, smiled and told me to get back up on the stool and give it another try. Embarrassed and angry, I brushed myself off, stood up, and placed the bucket back under Goldie's udder. Sitting back down on the stool, I followed Petie's instructions as he spoke softly and slowly to me.

Wrapping my thumb, forefinger, middle finger, and other forefinger around Goldie's teat, I squeezed and pulled down ever so slightly. To my astonishment a stream of warm milk squirted out and landed on Petie's green rubber milk boots, missing the bucket completely.

Satisfied I'd been successful in making milk come down, I patted Goldie on her hip, thanked her and told her she was a good cow. Returning my appreciative gesture with a snort, she slapped me across the face with her soiled, foul-smelling wet tail. For those who've never had the pleasure of being struck in the face by a cow tail meeting this description, it is akin to being hit with a mop that has been dragged through cow manure.

Determined to get through this, I wiped my face with my shirt sleeve, rinsed my hands in the bucket and tried again. Practicing my grip, heeding Petie's every word, I was soon milking with both hands.

If Grandpa could see me now!

Filling the bucket half-full, I walked to the house and showed Shelly what I'd done.

Milking Goldie every morning and evening after that provided us with enough milk to drink, supplement our farm animals' feed, and keep the stray cats satisfied that began appearing on the property.

Learning to live without electricity was a challenge, but we soon became accustomed to using lanterns. Fighting off mosquitoes, and looking for poisonous snakes in the black summer night, we carried our lanterns when walking the trail to the outhouse.

In the dead of winter, going outside with a lantern was an altogether different story. The cold biting winds often blew out the light, leaving us standing on hard frozen ground, shivering and returning to the house as quickly as we could.

Water for washing clothes and taking baths was pumped from a well, located 100 feet from the back of the house. Heating the water on the wood-burning stove in the front room, we kept a full kettle to rinse off after taking our baths. Shelly allowed the water to cool after bathing in the summer-time and used it to water the flowers.

Not having enough time to do our chores and bath for Sunday morning church services, we took our baths Saturday evenings. Filling a large, galvanized tub we bathed in the kitchen. Shelly hung a blanket in the doorway between the front room and kitchen for privacy, placed kitchen chairs around the tub and hung towels on them to keep the cool draft at bay as we bathed.

Shelly bathed Dakota first. Laughing and splashing water, he sometimes asked Tanner to get in the tub with him. Wrestling and playing games, they immersed themselves and saw who could blow the biggest bubbles. After Tanner and Dakota had taken their baths and emptied their dirty water, I re-filled the tub with clean, hot water for my bath. Bathing last, Shelly replenished the hot water and relaxed while Tanner, Dakota and I read or played games in the front room.

It is Amish custom to do laundry on Mondays. Filling two galvanized tubs half-full with hot water, Shelly placed a bar of lye soap and a washboard in the first tub. Scrubbing the clothes over the washboard, she rinsed them in the second tub and placed them in a basket to take outside. In the winter, as temperatures dropped into the teens, she took the frozen clothes off the line, hung them inside the house near the stove to dry and pressed them with the cast metal iron Katie had given her.

Summer is a busy season for the Amish. When I wasn't working with Eli and had caught up with my chores, I helped other Amish men on their farms. Alfalfa, ready for the first of several cuts, is dried and baled, straw is cut and stored in the barn. The cultivation of corn and potatoes continues and the threshing of small grains goes into late August.

It felt good to be part of the Amish family and community, a family who gives without expecting anything in return, and where mutual aid is a way of life. Our own family was coming together as well.

We felt renewed, restored, and emboldened.

9

A Wrestling Match And an Overturned Porta-Potty

Eli and I had just finished installing kitchen cabinetry in an Englishman's country home when he informed me that we'd be joining a crew to help finish a project in a small town nearby. My work thus far had been limited to measuring, cutting, and carrying pieces of material to him. I looked forward to the possibility of learning carpentry skills at the jobsite. Amish men are highly skilled carpenters and cabinet makers. I was excited about seeing their work first hand.

Arriving at the jobsite that Monday morning, I realized this was typical small town America, where values were clear, common sense ruled and the distinction between good and evil unmistakable. Town folk were dressed conservatively. Men wore long sleeve shirts buttoned to their neck, and tucked neatly into their pressed trousers. Town women donned full length dresses, summer hats, and slippers.

Many of the town's people had been slow to accept the Amish, so it caused quite a stir when a crew of Amish men, dressed in full black clothing, hats, and untrimmed beards, rode in on horse-drawn buggies. It was not as if the Amish men hadn't been to town before (*they had*), but they were usually accompanied by their wives and children.

Eli had a brief meeting with the crew, introduced me, and assigned me to work with a young man named David. Eli had told me on the way to town that David and his wife had been married several years but had remained childless. He said they'd tried to conceive, but finally agreed it was not God's will for them to have children.

David was quiet, keeping to himself during breaks. I couldn't help but feel compassion for him and hoped that I could somehow get to know him in time.

The job in town was to last another three weeks. Eli and I helped as we were needed and left the job site to start or finish other projects when it was necessary. Tanner kept the men entertained with humorous stories about the English world, constant pranks, and attempts at learning the German language.

Young Amish men enjoy competition and are formidable wrestlers, often having friendly scuffles at the beginning of a work day or during breaks. Winners of matches are never announced, as this would be considered "prideful," and contrary to Amish beliefs. Whenever the men were in town working, and tussled with each other, business owners and shoppers alike stopped what they were doing to cheer them on.

Tanner had wrestled in high school, had won numerous matches, and had pinned a few of the Amish men on the work crew. Noticing the ease with which he pinned some of the others, they told him Eli was the best wrestler in the Amish community, and that they should have a friendly go sometime.

It wasn't long before the men were teasing Tanner and Eli, saying they were going to have to see who could best the other. Eli attempted at first to laugh it off, but I could sense the competitive fire in him, and knew it wouldn't be long before he and Tanner would tangle.

Eli told the crew he and I would leave after lunch that Friday to finish installing cabinetry in a home a few miles away. The men began teasing Tanner. I joined in on the fun, telling him I'd seen Eli take a much larger Amish man down and pin him in seconds. I'd never seen Eli wrestle, but enjoyed riling Tanner, as he often did me. By the time lunch break came around, Tanner, normally in a jocular, teasing mood, was quiet and somber.

We sat on the ground, opened our paper lunch sacks, took out our sandwiches, and began eating. The typically talkative crew was quiet. One of the men spoke to Eli in German and snickered, looking at Tanner as he spoke. Eli answered him with a crooked smile, looked at Tanner and said, "The crew wants to see us wrestle."

Never one to refuse a challenge, Tanner rose to his feet and asked, "Now?"

"Yes," Eli replied, smiling wryly.

Eli knew if he refused to wrestle Tanner, he would never hear the end of it. He also knew, even though winners weren't announced at these matches, that he had never lost a match, and wasn't about to allow an Englishmen show him up in front of his men.

Tanner and Eli were similar in size, both standing 5' 9" tall, and weighing 160 pounds. I'd seen Tanner wrestle men from 140 pounds to 250 pounds, and had never seen him lose.

Tanner and Eli stood up and faced each other, bent their legs, squatted into position, stretched out their arms, locked hands, and began walking in a circling motion. Now on their feet, the crew started shouting directions to Eli in German, watching as the two men attempted to position themselves in a manner that would allow them to take the other down.

Tanner quickly loosened his grip, ducked his head and reached for Eli's right leg. Missing, he landed on all fours. Springing on his back, Eli shoved Tanner's head down with his left hand and tried to pull his right arm out from under him. Tanner rolled over quickly, jumped to his feet, and stood up. Eli followed suit. They faced each again, the determination on their faces evident as they locked hands, and began circling.

Eli feinted left at Tanner's head and went for his legs. Tanner leaped backward. They grabbed at each other's necks. Tanner dropped quickly to the ground, grabbed Eli's right leg, flipped him on his back and attempted to pin him. Eli wrapped his legs around Tanner's waist and threw him off. Time and again each wrestler attempted to put themselves into position to pin the other. Time and again they failed. It soon became apparent they were evenly matched.

Their bodies trembling, their chests heaving, they stopped, looked at each other, offered a faint smile, shook hands, and sat down, gasping for air.

Pleased at what they'd seen, the crew walked off, talking loudly about the moves Eli and Tanner had made, and how close the match had been. Onlookers who had gathered to watch, laughed and revisited the wrestler's moves as they went about their way.

Looking at me with disgust, Tanner tucked his shirt back into his pants, sneered and said, "Are you satisfied now, Bobby? I told you Eli couldn't pin me."

I finished my lunch, folded my paper bag, and put it in my back pocket. Noticing there was a line forming in front of the porta-potty, I walked over and stood in place. Working my way slowly to the front, I opened the door, dropped my pants, and sat on the cold, hard toilet seat.

Replaying the match in my mind's eye, enjoying the privacy of the outhouse, I began hearing the sound of laughter outside. Paying no mind, I went about my business when I felt the porta-potty beginning to bounce violently back and forth.

"Hey, what's going on?" I cried out, grabbing both sides of the toilet seat with everything I had, fearful of falling in.

I heard voices I didn't recognize as the shrill sounds of laughter grew louder, mixed with some of the Amish men's laughter.

The Amish enjoy playing tricks on each other, and will laugh and tease about it for weeks, often at inopportune times. They enjoy making up nicknames for each other about the way a young man's clothing may fit him, the shape of his body, or the length of his hair. They also enjoy other types of humor, which an Englishmen may find surprising to learn about from such "plain" people.

"Stop!" I shouted. "Whoever's doing that, stop it now! This thing's gonna' turn over," I screamed.

The porta-potty was now bouncing back and forth like a teeter totter about to come off its hinges.

"How do you like that?" Tanner shouted, laughing hysterically as he continued to shake the porta-potty.

"Is that you, Tanner? What are you doing?" I shouted, holding onto the sides of the toilet with both hands.

"Stop it! Are you crazy?"

Just as I was getting the last word out of my mouth, the porta-potty landed on its back with a great thud. Scrambling about, I crawled on my hands and knees, tried to open the door, only to discover it'd been locked.

"Let me out of here! Let me out of here now, Tanner!" I screamed in anger and embarrassment.

"Have you had enough?" Tanner screamed, pushing the porta-potty upright with the help of several others. Opening the door, holding his stomach with both hands, Tanner laughed out loud when he saw the look on my face.

"You could've killed me!" I shouted above the laughter, cleaning myself off, trying not to smile, as the English crowd walked away, shaking their heads their heads in amusement.

"I guess you won't tease me again, will you, Bobby?"

"I'll get you for this!" I said, walking back to pick up my tools and meet up with Eli, who was standing next to his buggy.

The man, who had sat on a bench outside the hardware store to watch the action got up and walked away. The woman, who had held a pretty piece of china in her hand and sat it down, gently picked it up and resumed shopping. The children who had stopped playing hop-scotch to watch, returned to their game. The excitement of the day was over. They would talk about this for weeks.

"Tanner's got a pretty mean temper, don't he?" Eli said, climbing into the buggy, snapping the reins.

"Yea, he can be pretty annoying at times," I said, smiling, inwardly satisfied that Eli had not been able to pin Tanner.

10
Samuel

I think of him often, and pray I'll see him again in heaven. His name was Samuel and he was the kindest, sweetest soul I've ever known. There are times I wished I had a picture of Samuel to take out of my wallet and look at when my heart is full of his dear memory. I long to see his face, but guess my mental image will have to suffice until we meet again.

Samuel was a widower, and the father of David, the Amish brother I'd worked with on the town project. Samuel's wife had been deceased several years when I met him. White-whiskered, frail, with sloping shoulders, arthritic hands, and ears a little too large for his head, Samuel looked as though he would break if one hugged him too hard.

Introducing himself after church one Sunday afternoon, he approached me and said, "I've always had a keen interest in the English, and the way they live. Would you like to come to my farm sometime for tea and a visit? We could talk about your experiences as an Englishmen. I'd like to hear some of your stories."

"I'd be happy to," I answered.

"And I'll be honored to share information with you about the Amish that I think would be most helpful to you and your family. I'll see you next Sunday then."

"I'll be there," I replied, watching as he climbed into his buggy, sat down on the hard wooden seat, snapped the reins lightly on the back of his aged, sway-backed, black gelding, and trotted away.

Friday afternoon as we were putting our tools away, I told Eli I was going to have tea with Samuel on Sunday and asked what he could tell me about him. Eli said Samuel had never remarried after his wife's death, that he enjoyed reading, and helping children with their school work.

He said Samuel had suffered from poor health for many years, and that his children kept his farm up for him.

"One day," Eli said, "Samuel's children will build a small house for him on their property, or he'll move in with one of them. Samuel is highly respected among the Amish for his knowledge of the world," Eli continued, stepping up to his buggy. "You'll enjoy your visit with him."

Work in August is slow for the Amish, as the bulk of their field work has been completed by this time of the year. Taking this opportunity to visit distant relatives, they hire English drivers known as "toots," to drive them where they'd like to go.

One of the stipulations of the *Ordnung*, the governing rules of the Amish church, is that they cannot own a vehicle, but they can ride in one. Even this means of conveyance was denied to Samuel as his increasingly poor health did not allow it. His traveling days were over. His journeys were now limited to reading the English newspaper, or looking through travel magazines, which he enjoyed immensely.

Sunday came quickly. I crawled out of bed, washed my face, put on my clothes, and walked outside to greet the still morning air. The days were growing hot and humid by mid-afternoon. I planned to eat breakfast, hitch up Maggie to the buggy, and spend a few hours with Samuel before the afternoon sun had a chance to blister my neck and arms.

Samuel opened the front door and asked me to come in. I followed him inside, hung my hat on a hook and sat down in a large comfortable rocking chair. A *Book of Martyrs* sat on a table next to a partially folded quilt. A Bible rested on a rocking chair across the room. A thin red cloth book marker hung loosely from its pages.

Excusing himself, Samuel stepped into the kitchen and returned carrying two cups of hot tea, his hands trembling as he re-entered the room. I couldn't help but think, as I took the cup from his hand and placed it on a nearby table that I'd been there before: another time, another life.

My mind went back to Grandpa and Grandma Bolin's farm house. I remembered the smell of grandma's freshly washed and ironed dress, her hair in a tight bun, pinned behind her head, the fragrance of grandpa's Old Spice aftershave lotion. The distinct and familiar scent of their home that even today takes me back to the sweet memories of being there. I looked down at the hardwood floors and across the room at the wooden rocking chair where Samuel sat, almost expecting to see Grandpa sitting there, his Bible in his hand.

"I'm glad you came," Samuel said in a whisper, picking up the Bible from his rocking chair and placing it on his lap as he sat in his rocker. "I heard about you from a few of the church members. My son David said you and he worked together on the new store in town. Tell me about your family," he said, leaning slightly forward in his chair.

"My dad's family lives in Arkansas. His oldest brother Jack is a farmer, and Crittenden County Judge. Two of his other brothers are truck drivers. Another brother owns a restaurant. Dad's two sisters are housewives."

"Are your father's family members Christian?"

"They're believers, but seldom attend church."

"What about your mother's family?"

"Mother's father is a church pastor, and three of her brothers are also pastors.

"And your family?" Samuel asked.

"I have three children from a previous marriage."

"You must miss them terribly?"

"I do. The pain is sometime more than I can bear."

"Bless your heart. I will pray, and ask God to give you and your family strength in this matter.

Tell me about your grandfather, the pastor."

"Grandpa Bolin is my best friend. He understands me. He doesn't always approve of the things I do, but is there when I need him. We read the Bible together. He explains things to me that I don't understand."

"How wonderful of him to see you through life's difficult and trying times. You must love him dearly."

"I do."

I told Samuel the story of how, as a nine year old boy, I rose from my bed in our Memphis home, washed my face, slipped on my Sunday clothes, slicked down my hair the way mother taught me, and tip-toed out the front door. Of making my way outside, walking down the long, graveled driveway onto James Road, and into the Baptist Church to find the pastor.

"Can I help you, son?' the pastor asked, looking down at me with curious eyes.

"My grandpa told me I needed to be baptized!" I said matter-of-factly, grinning through two missing front teeth."

"He did now!" the pastor replied.

"Yes sir. That's what my grandpa told me!" I said, looking up proudly, squaring my shoulders.

Mother had taught my sisters and me to always say, "Yes, Sir" and "Yes, Ma'am" when speaking to adults, saying it showed respect to our elders.

"Grandpa said I can't get into heaven if I don't get baptized, and I want to get to heaven… cuz my grandpa's gonna be there!"

"You don't say? Is that why you're here today? To be baptized?"

"Yes sir. So when can I be baptized? I need to get home soon cuz I think my momma and daddy might be awake, and I'm sure they'll be worried about me when they can't find me!"

"Well hold on a minute young man! What's your name?"

"Bobby. Bobby Brawley!"

"Well, Bobby Brawley. How old are you?"

"Nine, sir," I replied, standing up straight like grandpa told me, tucking my shirt into my loose corduroy pants.

"Tell me, how did you get here, Bobby?"

"I walked, all by myself!" I said proudly.

Introducing himself as Pastor Williams, he said he would include my name on the list of people being baptized after church and asked me to sit in the front pew next to Ms. Williams.

Returning to the pulpit, he delivered his sermon, announced it was time for the baptisms to begin, and summoned me forward. I wondered, as I walked slowly to the stage, if Mother and Dad had realized I was gone and if they did, if they were mad at me. The pastor asked me to sit on a hard wooden chair, placed a light cloth around my shoulders, and introduced me to the congregation.

"Dear brothers and sisters. I'd like you to meet Bobby Brawley," he said in a loud, commanding voice. "Bobby has come to church this beautiful Sunday morning to be baptized."

A soft hush ran through the enormous building. I watched as church members cupped their hands and whispered into each other's ears.

What are they saying about me? I wondered.

Shrinking down in the chair I tried to make myself invisible.

The pastor began reading from the Bible, and as he spoke, gently sprinkled water over my head. Asking church members to pray with him, he finished and asked if I had accepted the Lord God in my life.

"Yes, sir," I whispered, smiling faintly.

I wasn't exactly sure what "accepting God into my life" meant, but knew it was something I had to do.

Removing the cloth from my shoulders, the pastor asked me to return to my seat. As I stood up and began walking down the steps, I felt like I was walking on air, as if I were weightless, the pastor's words still ringing in my ears.

Opening the front door to our home that afternoon after church I saw Mother sitting on the couch, her face buried in her hands, sobbing.

"Where've you been?" she cried out, hearing me step onto the hardwood floor.

"I got baptized!" I said, grinning widely, hoping my news would spare me a whippin'.

"You walked all the way to church by yourself?" she asked, trying to contain her emotions. "That church is over a mile away, Bobby. Your father and I have been worried sick about you!"

Reaching out with both arms, she pulled me close to her body. I felt her body tremble and her warm tears fall gently on the top of my head.

"Don't you ever do that again! Do you hear what I'm saying to you, Bobby?"

"Yes ma'am. I hear you. I promise I will never, ever, do that again."

Pulling away slowly, I walked into my bedroom, closed the door behind me, looked into the mirror above my dresser and smiled.

Grandpa's going to be so proud of me, I thought to myself, taking off my Sunday clothes, feeling closer to him than I ever had. The desire to be baptized had been instilled in me the first time I had heard him preach about how important it was, and what it meant to be a Christian. Likewise, my desire to join the Amish came from a need to get back to a simple, honest, straightforward and humble way of life.

"What a wonderful story, Bob. Your father and mother must have been very proud of you. I've heard stories of English divorces and of how hurtful and destructive they can be to families. I've also read of prisons where lost souls scream in the night, longing to be with their loved ones and of young people running in gangs, killing each other over drugs, money, power and greed. Our children are taught to walk in righteousness, be obedient to their elders, and not to harm one another."

Samuel rose, took our cups to the kitchen and asked if I'd like to join him outside. He continued, sitting under the dappled shade of an elm tree, "The Amish believe in keeping the old ways, and that to accept new ways would be to invite the devil into their homes. Unlike many English churches we don't gather our spirituality or put it together for our personal use. We see it as a priceless legacy that has been intertwined over several hundreds of years of observance. And unlike others when faced with painful and trying situations, we respond with grace, love, acceptance and understanding. When an Amish family is in need, we do not ask for outside help, but instead help each other. To accept help from the government would be to deny our faith that God will provide for us."

Samuel told me of being sickly as a child, and of how he spent every free moment reading about people in faraway places, yearning to learn more about their lives and their cultures. The late morning air began to warm and become heavy. I could see Samuel beginning to tire, his frail body wilting. I thanked him for inviting me to his home and shook his trembling hand. Looking into his fading hazel eyes, I wished I could've taken that moment and pressed it between the pages of a treasured book so I could take it out and touch it again.

Throughout the time I spent with the Amish, Samuel and I remained close friends. He stopped often at our farm for tea, sharing stories of his wife, children, and grandchildren. I found it incredulous as to how he remembered the names and ages of his many grandchildren and great-grandchildren, what chores they performed, who was dating whom, and who had "quit" whom. He took great pride in the fact that, even though his body had failed him, his mind was as keen as ever.

Holding Dakota on his lap, he sang German hymns, taught him simple German words, and told him childhood stories. Samuel appeared to have a great affinity for Shelly and treated her with the utmost respect. Complimenting her cooking, and the way she kept house, he often told me how much she reminded him of his beloved wife. He once told me what mattered most to Amish families was not wealth or status, but that the man was a good provider, and the wife, a good help-mate.

"The rest," he continued, "will take care of itself. People go hungry and sometimes starve in the city, but the Amish will never go without food as long as they're willing to work hard on their farms."

He frequently talked about the changes affecting their community, the price of hay, feed, how the cattle and pig markets were changing, and the resulting impact these things had on their families.

Samuel lived a righteous life, and instilled quiet resolution in others. He saw the world through the eyes of the common man, and was not interested in power or prestige. His time on earth will be measured by the many lives he touched, his stories, and his everlasting friendship.

I think of him often, and miss him dearly.

11

Church Life and Rituals

Customs of one church district in an Amish community may vary widely, or ever so slightly from another. While one group in Pennsylvania or Indiana may embrace a particular style, color of clothing, or the manner in which that clothing is worn, a group in Missouri or Kansas might choose to alter or completely avoid these rituals.

Likewise, one group may choose to cover their buggies and have rubber tires on their wheels, while another group may feel this too "worldly." An Amish settlement consists of families living in close proximity to one other. Settlements are typically small, but can be quite large.

A church district or congregation is a sacramental group of members encircling an area inside a settlement. Church membership is determined by how many members can fit into a farm house or barn. Being a self-governing body, ceremonial and institutional affairs are reinforced during church services.

Church district boundaries are decided by leaders and members. Members and their families are strongly urged to attend services in their district; that being their "home church." Moreover, church attendance is mandatory, unless you are sick. Rituals such as weddings, funerals and barn raisings extend beyond these boundaries.

The Old Order Amish classify group members as "high" or "low," depending upon their extent of worldliness, low-church being the most plain, or least ostentatious, while high church members operate in a more relaxed manner. Interaction between these two groups is highly unlikely.

It was after we'd been accepted by the Missouri Old Order Amish that I was told that the bishop had made an exception by allowing my family to live in their settlement. We began attending church shortly after my meeting with him.

The sight of dozens of black, topless, buggies filled with families of all ages, forming a single line, and the sound of hooves on the hard dirt was an experience I will never forget.

I had no preconceived ideas about what church services might entail, and the fact that they would be spoken in the German language had completely escaped me. Church Sundays were spent hurrying through breakfast, feeding the animals, milking the cow, hitching up Maggie to the buggy, and making sure everyone looked presentable.

Baths were taken the night before, and clothes laid out over the chairs. Having no mirrors to check ourselves out, everyone took turns standing in front of each other asking, "How do I look?"

I don't think Shelly ever got used to living without a mirror.

Church members helped families holding services in their homes by cleaning stables, rearranging furniture and baking meals and pies. Performing the bulk of the work, women rearranged furniture, used a special polish to blacken the stoves, (*due to the color being burned off while cooking,)* and washed the china while men folk gathered benches, supervised seating and acted as ushers. Church services began at nine, lasted until noon, and starting with hymns lasting as long as twenty-five minutes. Immediately following the hymns was a preliminary sermon, followed by a silent prayer.

Standing while the deacon read from the Bible, members then sat during the main sermon, which is followed by the reading of another chapter from the Bible. Other ministers attending the service give "testimonies" at the behest of the preacher. The preacher then gave his closing remarks. At that time each member turned and knelt while the preacher read a prayer. The Benediction was then offered.

We listened as he spoke softly, in a monotone voice:

"Finally, dear brethren, rejoice, be perfect, be comforted and be of one mind; be peaceful, and the God of love and peace shall be with you. Greet each other with the Holy Kiss. You are greeted by all the saints. (II Cor. 13:11 – 13)

So I submit myself, with you, to God and his gracious hand, that He be pleased to keep us in the saving faith, to strengthen us in it, to guide and lead us until a blessed end; and all this through Jesus Christ. Amen."

As the preacher said "Jesum Christum" at the end of the church service, members would bend down on their knees. The place where the next meeting was announced, the closing hymn was sung, and dismissal took place with the youngest leaving first.

Unlike other churches I'd attended, where the "spirit" often times grips and consumes the service, everything in the Amish church has a well-established order to it. Ordained men, older men, and middle-aged men enter the house first, followed by women with small children and unmarried boys. Men sat on one side of the house, while women and children sat on the opposite side of the room. After church, meals were served in the following order; men, women, small children and unmarried boys.

Sitting quietly, listening for German words I'd learned, my mind drifted to Sunday services at grandpa's church. Wearing freshly ironed "church" clothes, I sat in Sunday school, hoping the teacher wouldn't call on me and, afraid someone would hear me sing, mouthed words as the choir sang hymnals.

I looked forward to seeing grandpa standing at the podium, and watched with anticipation as he raised his Bible toward the rafters. Waving it frantically back and forth above his head, he told us we were all sinners and were going to hell if we didn't change our ways.

"The world may change," he shouted, pacing side to side, looking out over the small congregation, "but the Word of God never will!"

I listened to his every word, and watched as grandma sat in the front pew, affirming him with an occasional "Yes, praise the Lord, thank you Jesus!"

Sitting through Amish services on hard, backless benches through spiritless songs, dry testaments and long, monotonous sermons, I waited for a display of emotion, the lifting of a hand, an emotional voice, supporting the bishop's sermon. Instead, members sat quietly and motionless, fanning themselves, wiping their brow, tending to a child, or swatting flies.

As much as I loved and admired grandpa, I was never fully comfortable when members began speaking in tongues or getting "slain in the spirit." It wasn't that I disagreed with their behavior or doubted their sincerity, I just felt awkward, and uncomfortable. Slipping outside when no one was looking, I opened the door to our car, listened from afar, and waited for the front doors to open, signaling that church services were over.

So there I was, spiritually somewhere in between church worship styles, where members are encouraged on one hand to get in the spirit and get "happy," and on the other hand, participating in church services where members are expected to be quiet, still, and non-participative.

I found myself feeling I didn't have a true comfort level in either setting.

Visiting with other Amish families at the after service meal we talked about the weather, crops, work, new babies, and discreetly discussed who was "going" with whom. The afternoon fellowship typically ended between two and three o'clock. At this time, family members climbed in their wagons and left for home to perform their evening chores. Teenagers, wishing to attend evening hymn singing stayed behind, visited, and helped set up for the event.

"Does Tanner plan to join the church?" Rebecca Yoder asked, turning to Shelly.

Rebecca's seventeen-year-old daughter, Edna, had shown interest in Tanner. His good looks, personality, playful ways, and availability had been the subject of many whispered conversations among young Amish maids and their mothers.

"We don't know for certain what Tanner's going to do. He's still trying to make up his mind," replied Shelly.

"Well, he'll be making a decision soon, I reckon," Rebecca stated, matter of factly.

"I reckon," Shelly replied, turning to me with a subtle wink and a smile.

12

A Beautiful Bay and a Buggy Race

Jacob had told me I'd have to return Maggie as soon I found a replacement for her, and that I should check with Eli to see if he knew anyone who might have a buggy horse for sale. Checking with Eli the following week, he told me he wasn't aware of any, and advised me to check the auction. He said if I found a good horse he would train it when he had the time.

I had a picture in my mind of the horse I wanted. He would be young, tall, angular, well-built, and have good trotter potential. Amish children are raised to be humble, but every young Amish man takes pleasure, and pride, in knowing his buggy and horse are admired by young men and women alike. It was common knowledge that teenage boys spoke secretly of the beautiful Standardbred trotters they saw in racing magazines at the downtown drugstore. Eli's stud had come from a well-known horse breeder in Indiana, and was the unstated pride of the community.

Walking past the stalls as they sold cattle in the main arena, looking for a horse that might catch my eye, I spotted one of the most magnificent animals I'd ever seen. Prancing, snorting, neighing, and throwing his head side to side, his full, luxurious mane rippled, and his high-stepping action was worthy of a military parade.

A dark bay, standing sixteen hands tall with a broad forehead, small pointed ears, large eyes and nostrils and a small muzzle, he was handsome beyond compare. His powerful, thick beautifully arched neck and long black tail were carried high as he stopped, snorted loudly, and pranced stiff-legged to the stall door bars where I was standing in awe.

Reaching through the bars, I gently touched his nose. He shuddered, offered a subtle whinny and shook his head. Our eyes locked. We stood still, looking into each other's souls. A sense of something I'd never before experienced came over me. It was as if I could feel his power rushing into my body and spirit. I felt, for a brief moment, as if we'd become one.

I can't afford this horse, I said to myself. *Someone will buy him and make a champion race horse out of him. I need to keep looking.*

Stroking his nose and forehead, all I could think about was hitching him to my buggy, pulling up at church on Sunday mornings and watching men of all ages look at him with great envy. I could see the look on Eli's face as he turned to see what all the commotion was about, his eyes settling on him, when he first saw...Comet.

Yeah, that's what I'll name him, Comet.

Walking past a few more stalls I returned to the bleachers, sat down and waited. After several older horses, a mule, and a burro passed through the ring, the doors swung open and a man, doing all he could do to keep the bay from running over him, led him into the arena.

Excitement filled the air. Bidders stood up in their seats to watch this imposing, beautiful animal. The bay strutted around the arena, his head and tail held head high, his thick black hooves seemingly not touching the sawdust floor.

"Hold it folks! What in the world do we have here! Where did this beautiful animal come from? Watch him boys! He's a rogue and a rounder! Can I get a bid on this beautiful three-year-old thoroughbred bay? He's not been broke folks, and will need a lot of training, but will make someone a nice horse. Who'll start the bid? A hundred dollars! Who'll open the bid at a hundred dollars?"

Not a soul raised his card. I was stunned. It appeared that no one was interested in the bay. Could this be possible? Why wasn't anyone bidding on him? Did they know something that I didn't?

"Seventy five dollars! Can I get someone to open the bid at seventy five dollars on this stunning bay horse?" the auctioneer shouted into the microphone.

No response...

"Fifty dollars, I'll give you fifty dollars for him!" an Englishmen sitting in the front row shouted, lifting his card.

"Sixty five dollars!" a shout came from across the building.

"Well, alright, we might get this horse sold yet!" the auctioneer exclaimed. "We have a sixty five dollar bid!"

"One hundred dollars," I yelled, raising my card high, waving it in the air.

You could have heard a pin drop.

"We have a hundred dollar bid. Who'll give me a hundred and twenty five dollars?"

"A hundred and fifteen dollars, and that's as high as I'll go," the first bidder shouted.

"We have a bid for a hundred and fifteen dollars! Can I get a hundred and twenty five dollars? Who'll give me a hundred and twenty five dollars for this exquisite animal?'"

I raised my card.

"One hundred and twenty five dollars, I have a bid for one hundred and twenty five dollars. Are there any other bids?" the announcer cried out.

Silence...

My pulse escalated. My hair stood on end. I wondered if others sitting around me could hear the pounding of my heart.

"Okay then, hearing no other bids, going once, going twice, and going---three times! Sold to number twelve," he shouted, pointing toward me.

Oh my God, I thought. *I've just bought the horse of my dreams, and all I can do is sit here, frozen to my chair, trembling. Where's Jacob? I need Jacob!*

"That's a fine looking animal you bought, sir. Please pay the cashier at the window," the clerk said, walking up the bleachers, sitting next to me.

Coming to my senses, I walked down the steps in a daze,

concentrating on each step I took, careful not to fall. I paid the cashier and hired a driver to transport the bay back to the farm that afternoon.

I watched with excitement and a fair amount of trepidation, as the driver led the massive bay to the trailer, walked him up the ramp, and locked the metal door behind him. Reaching in and patting him on his neck, I was excited to get him home, into my barn, and in his stall.

Eli stopped by a few days later. Unlatching the door and entering the stall, he looked at Comet, looked back at me and said, "We don't see many horses like this around these parts, Bob," gently patting Comet's rump, checking his conformation.

"He's awfully young. He could be a real handful. I wonder if you're ready for a horse like this."

Eli's comments stung. My English pride, rising to the surface, got in the way of common sense. *I'll show him,* I thought to myself. *I'll train Comet, and he'll be as good as any horse he's ever trained, as good as any horse in the county.*

Unlatching the stall door and stepping outside, Eli gave me step-by-step instructions as to how to train Comet. Watching as he backed his big stud out on the lane, snapped a sharp command and charged away, I suddenly felt weak in the knees.

Was buying Comet a mistake? Should I have waited? I wondered, as I walked back to the barn.

I trained Comet to the buggy over the next few weeks, following Eli's instructions to the word. Then the day came to take him on his maiden voyage. Harnessing him early one morning after chores, I climbed in the buggy, took the reins firmly in both hands, took a deep breath, and gave him the order to drive.

Pricking his ears, he took a step forward, pulled the buggy slowly across the gravel drive, pulled out on the lane and broke into a brisk trot. We spent the next hour driving up the lane and back to the farm, stopping, starting, and backing up.

The following Sunday I backed Comet up to the buggy, harnessed him, and asked Shelly and Dakota to get in. Saying a silent prayer, I took a deep breath, snapped the reins, and headed for church.

"You did it, Dad, you did it!" exclaimed Dakota.

"Not so loud." Shelly whispered, sighing heavily, clasping her hands, holding them up as if in prayer. "You'll scare him."

Coming home from church that afternoon, the steady panting of Comet's breath communicated a tremulous motion to the buggy. Listening to the tramping of his hooves as they struck the hardened road and the jingling of the harness, I felt a strong sense of pride and accomplishment. I had taken a raw, unbroken, three-year-old stud horse and turned him into a fine-tuned working animal, one which would make any Amish man proud.

It was on a church Sunday, as we were taking a slow jog back to the farm, when a group of Amish teens passed our buggy. Looking back and pointing behind us, they shouted "Macht Schnell! Eli! Macht Schnell!"

I glanced back to see Eli's buggy gaining on me. Sitting up straight, I gave Comet a slap on his rump with the reins. Startled, he raised his head, pricked his ears forward, stretched out his long body, and began taking great long strides.

The race was on...

"What are you doing?" Shelly shouted, grabbing my arm, her eyes growing as big as saucers.

"Eli's trying to pass me!" I yelled, looking backwards, and then at her.

Quickly looking behind us, she cupped her hands over her bonnet.

"Beat him, Bobby!" Shelly screamed, smiling, and giving me a mischievous look.

I had read that a good Standardbred's trot was faster than a nonracing horse's gallop. I believed it that day as Eli and I raced down the back country road, having the time of our lives and headed, unbeknownst to us, straight into trouble.

Eli, his stud at full stride, pulled next to me, smiled, tipped his hat, and gently pulled back on the reins. I tugged on Comet's reins and slowed him down.

A few days later, as I sat at the table eating breakfast, I heard a knock at the front door and saw Jacob standing on our porch. His head lowered, he was pacing back and forth, looking at his buggy, then back at our front door.

"Hello," I said, opening the door, sensing by the look on his face something was wrong.

"Can you walk with me to my buggy?" he asked.

"Sure."

Standing next to his buggy, leaning against the steps, Jacob informed me that the bishop had heard about Eli's and my display of speed. He said the bishop was very unhappy with the both of us, and had asked him to share his concern. He said the bishop wanted to make it very clear that this sort of thing would never happen again, and if it did, there would be serious repercussions.

I thanked Jacob for stopping by and asked him to please assure the bishop that I'd learned my lesson. That afternoon after supper I walked out to the barn, fed Comet an extra-large can of grain, and whispered into his ear how proud I was of him.

Many changes had occurred in my life since I had joined the Amish. Changes I gladly accepted, but as I stood there brushing Comet, recalling how exciting my race with Eli had been, I smiled, and thought to myself, *Man, that was fun…*

13

A Summer Storm And a Barn-Raising

Summer was in full swing. Eli and I were working fourteen hour days at jobs throughout the county, installing cabinets, and working construction jobs wherever we were needed. Stopping at a large Amish farm one morning to look at a job we were met by Amos Yoder.

A short, stocky man with thick legs and tiny feet, his white beard contrasted with a ruddy red complexion. I later learned his complexion was the result of his love of elderberry wine, which he made himself and kept stocked in his cellar.

Amos and his wife Fannie, had twelve children, ranging from their oldest daughter Emma, to their youngest son, Johnny. Their two-story farmhouse sat off the state highway and was surrounded by lush green pasture, beautiful white fencing, and numerous outbuildings. Rows of beautifully colored flowers filled the flower beds at the entrance to their house.

Teaching children to work and accept responsibility is very important to the Amish. Following that tradition, Amos taught his children to help out on the farm. Starting as early as four years of age, his boys learned to feed chickens and calves, gather eggs and drive horses. Likewise, Fannie taught the girls to prepare meals, weed the garden, milk cows, feed the horses, wash, and hang out clothes.

Amos's farm was the envy of every Amish and non-Amish farmer in the county. He raised corn, oats, rye, and hay crops for feeding animals and kept a large garden. He also kept beef, dairy cattle, hogs, poultry, and sheep. It was not uncommon to see townspeople's cars parked in the long drive to his farm, looking to buy fresh vegetables and meat, or simply admiring his property. Amos had a drive and business sense about him few Amish men in this small settlement had, and although it went unspoken, some members looked at his family somewhat differently than they did other families. While many family farms in the community struggled, Amos's farm flourished.

After looking at the job site Amos asked us to come in the house and have a glass of homemade wine. He told me he'd heard good things about me, wanted to know how we were doing, and told me if I ever needed anything to let him know. Amos and I became close friends. I visited him often at his farm, helping with chores and asking for advice when I needed someone to talk to about farming, about life, and about family.

Returning home that afternoon after visiting Amos's farm, I saw steel-gray clouds roiling in the western sky, and watched as they darkened, and became an angry greenish-purple color. I quickly put Comet away, ran into the house and closed the door behind me.

"Looks like a bad one comin' this way," I said to Shelly, peering out a kitchen window as large drops of rain begin to splat against the panes. The wind began to pick up and howl over the barn roof, followed by a rapid-fire barrage of rain and then a virtual downpour.

Dakota leaped out of his bed and into my lap as the sounds of rolling thunder, screaming winds and broken tree branches somersaulted against the weather-beaten house. I couldn't help but wonder what we would do if the roof were to blow off, or a wall were to collapse.

The torrential rain eased off briefly, and then began pouring again, collecting into large pools around the farmhouse. The second floor of the weathered house began to shimmy and groan. Something large smashed against the outside wall and broke into pieces. A piece of flying debris broke a front room window, Dakota scooched close to me. I could only imagine the damage the storm was doing to our garden.

The hazed figure of a horse-drawn buggy came slowly through the blinding rain and stopped in front of our farm house. A moment later I heard a voice crying, "Help me, Bobby, please help me!" Not believing what I'd heard, I jumped out of my rocker, ran to the window, and looked out to see Tanner standing in the pouring rain. Maggie's chest, body and feet were dripping with mud. Holding his hand against the metal gate, Tanner looked at me with an expression of sheer terror, his body convulsing as if in a fit.

"Help me!" he screamed again. "Help me!"

I ran to the door, threw it open and yelled, "Let go of the gate!"

"I can't!" he cried out, his face ridden with anguish and despair.

Running to him and wrapping my arms around his body, I pulled with all my strength, but could not budge him.

"Let go!" I shouted, wiping the drenching rain from my eyes.

Tanner appeared to be helpless, his face was red, his hair and clothes sopping wet, his eyes fixed in a trance.

What will I tell his family? How will I explain this to them? I wondered, thinking he'd been struck by lightning.

Wrapping my arms around his body and clasping my hands together, I jerked again with everything I had. His grip finally broken, we fell to the ground and landed in a huge puddle of water, splashing mud in our eyes, hair, and on our clothes.

"C'mon," I shouted, lifting him up, "let's get inside!"

"What?" he yelled.

"C'mon!" I screamed. "Let's go!"

Looking up at me through drenched, smiling eyes and a wicked look on his face, he pushed me away, laughed like a man possessed and shouted, "I gotcha, Bobby! I gotcha! I can't believe it, I gotcha!"

"I'll kill you!" I screamed, grabbing him around the neck and throwing him to the ground.

We rolled in the mud, laughing and wrestling like two little boys experiencing their first mud puddle. He broke loose, ran to the house, slammed the front door behind him and shouted, "Hide me Shelly, hide me! Bobby's trying to kill me!"

Standing in the front room, staring at each other, both covered in mud, we laughed until we cried as the deluge outside continued. I promised I'd pay him back one day, but knew in my heart I wouldn't. I was just happy he was alive, and that God had seen fit to keep His eye on my family through this violent storm.

A few weeks later, Eli told me of a young Amish family needing to have a barn built and asked if I'd like to help out, saying attending a barn-raising would be a good opportunity for our family to meet other church members and show support for them. At these barn raisings, men help out by building and restoring buildings, splitting wood, erecting out-buildings, painting, fencing and butchering. Women gather to quilt, sew and bake on special occasions such as church gatherings, weddings and funerals. If a person in the community is sick everyone knows about it and sees to it that they are well taken care of.

It was a beautiful late summer day when we arrived at Levi and Susie Hilty's farm. Newly married, they were in need of a barn to house the farm animals they'd received from the Amish community. Shelly, Dakota, and I had gotten up early, taken care of our chores and hooked Comet up for the two mile trip. Stepping up to the buggy, Shelly placed the large bean salad she'd made the night before in Dakota's lap for safekeeping. I saw twenty buggies parked in the dirt lane along a fenced pasture as we came over the knoll on the east side of the farm.

Women sat on benches above the site where the barn was to be built, watching their children as they played in the fields and around the farm house. Young unmarried men, lacking skills to construct buildings, carried lumber, nails and other items to the work site.

Master Amish carpenters had laid out the plans and ordered the material well ahead of time for the project. Blocks and cement used for the barn's foundation were laid out the day before. The plan for the day was to construct the wood frame structure with the remainder of the barn to be built over the next few weeks. With the community providing the labor and supplying the material to build the barn, the Hilty family would get off to a good start.

Tanner, visiting with Mandy and some of her friends, took off his straw hat and waved eagerly as we pulled up. I stopped, tethered Comet to the back of another buggy and joined the others.

Excited and somewhat overwhelmed by the number of Amish families I'd not yet met, I began looking for a familiar face and spotted Eli standing in a crowd with a few of the men I'd worked with on a previous project. Shelly and Dakota joined Katie on a bench and were introduced to several women she'd not yet met.

I left Shelly and walked to the area where Eli and the others were and listened as they talked about what was going to take place and who was going to work with whom.

"Bob, you'll work with me, David, and Tanner, building walls, and lifting them into place," Eli said.

We quickly began putting the floor together and helping others hammer and build walls. Taking a short break later that morning I walked up the hill where Shelly and other Amish women were sitting and watched as men, looking like ants on a picnic sandwich, swarmed over the rising building and the surrounding ground.

Carrying lumber, sawing, lifting walls and hammering, they worked together like pieces of a fine-tuned clock. I took a drink of water and ran back down just in time to help raise the south wall. Holding it up as another group of men joined it to the east wall, I felt a strong sense of accomplishment. I'd never known the sensation of standing together with a group of men and feeling as though I had a right to be there, to know that I belonged.

Working until late afternoon, I saw something of a miracle that day. Men, women and children coming together to help a neighbor in need, singing hymns, laughing, and enjoying themselves as they worked in unison toward a common goal. Returning home a little before dark I put Comet away, fed the animals, watered the garden, and sat alone on the grass near the pond, listening to the sounds of summer, replaying the day's events in my mind. I'd never before, and have not since, experienced the feeling of love, respect, and fellowship I felt as I watched the barn take shape that day.

I read somewhere that the Amish may be the only honest and true Christians left in the modern world. I don't know about that, and will leave others to debate it, but I do know that the Missouri Old Order Amish are the closest thing to saints I've ever known.

I'm a retired facilities director now and have often thought, as I sat in meetings between union representatives and management, trying to settle employer-employee conflicts, of how much better this world would be if we could all work together as well as the Amish did the day they raised the Hilty barn.

14

Amish Love Triangle

Emma hadn't been to church singings for over a year. She'd been caring for her bedridden mother which took most of her time, but now that her mother was in the hospital she decided to attend the Sunday evening singing and meet the handsome young Englishmen she'd heard so much about.

She arrived in her buggy that evening, greeted friends and noticed Mandy Beiler talking to an Amish man she'd not yet met. Looking him over from afar, she decided this must be the fella causing all the commotion. Tying off her horse, she walked towards a gathering of teens standing outside the Schwartz farm house. Tanner, standing next to Mandy, noticed her walking their way and looked surreptitiously over Mandy's shoulder as she drew nearer.

"So you're Tanner," Emma said.

"I guess so!" Tanner replied, with a huge smile.

"Pleased to meet you, I'm Emma Yoder, daughter of Amos and Fannie Yoder."

Mandy, noticing the eye contact and mutual attraction between the two, took Tanner by the arm and said, "We should go inside. The others will be waiting for us."

Sitting across the table from each other during singing Emma passed flirtatious glances Tanner's way. Tanner returned them, trying not to attract Mandy's attention. Later that evening, during breaks between songs, he attempted to get close to Emma but his efforts were thwarted at every turn by Mandy's watchful eye.

Catching up on the latest news after singing, teens began leaving for home. Morning chores awaited them and there was no snooze alarm on the Old English Game Rooster whose boisterous crows awoke them bright and early each morning.

Emma, noticing Mandy was inside helping the elders clean up, strolled quietly up to Tanner as he climbed into his buggy.

"I hope to see you again," she said, placing her hand gently on his.

"I hope so too," Tanner replied.

"Gute Nacht."

"Good night."

Tanner took Mandy home that evening. He liked Mandy. He'd liked her from the day he'd first seen her standing in the Beiler doorway. But meeting Emma had stirred feelings inside of him, feelings he could not ignore.

Stopping alongside the road, he took Mandy's face in his hands and gave her a soft peck on her lips.

"Is something wrong?" she asked.

"Everything's fine," he replied, looking longingly at the full moon and then at the shadows along the hollow ridge on the road.

He'd been serious about courting Mandy, but now, having looked into Emma's eyes, his mind was filled with doubt.

"I'd better get you home. Your parents will be worried."

Awakened by the sweet aroma of frying bacon, Tanner flung the quilt off his body, climbed out of bed, put his clothes on and rushed through breakfast. He'd thought about Emma all night, even dreamed of her. He made up his mind, as he rushed through chores, that he was going to take a buggy ride and see if she'd like to go on a picnic with him.

Packing two sandwiches, a jar of applesauce, napkins, spoons, and a Mason jar of water in a paper sack, he harnessed his bay gelding and began the two mile drive to the Yoder farmhouse. He couldn't help but think, as he neared the Yoder drive, of the changes that had occurred in his life since coming to the Amish settlement. Of how different Mandy and Emma were from the English girls he'd dated.

Lying in bed that morning, Emma looked up at the tall ceiling and bare white walls of her second-story bedroom. She rose, dressed herself, and couldn't help but wonder if Tanner had felt the same thing she'd felt when their eyes met and when she'd touched his hand.

Her awakening mind wandered to her mom, and for a moment she started toward her bedroom to check on her. As thoughts fell into place, she remembered she was not there, but was in the hospital.

Opening the window, she pushed the white, neatly pressed, cotton curtains back. It'd been a long time since she'd allowed herself to think of her own needs, of her life, and of her future. She was twenty-one. Most of her friends were married and had begun their own families.

When will I be married? She wondered.

Looking out over the pasture, allowing the cool breeze to blow through her uncapped hair, she suddenly felt alive. She smiled as she watched her younger brothers chase each other around the barn. It seemed like it'd been an eternity since she'd taken the time to enjoy the morning. Humming her favorite hymn, she walked down the steps and wondered what she would do this bright, beautiful, sunny day.

Mandy had decided, after putting it off for weeks that today would be the day she'd talk to her mother about her feelings for Tanner. Katie was well aware of the physical attraction between the two, which awakened a nagging concern as to whether Mandy might one day leave the Amish faith.

Mandy had shown a keen interest in the English ways since she was a small girl. Later, working as a maid in English homes, she'd often come home singing English tunes she'd heard on the radio. Suspecting Mandy had worn makeup outside the home, Katie had found lipstick and rouge under her pillow, as well as handwritten notes from English boys.

"I love Tanner," Mandy said, sitting at the table across from her Katie.

"I know you do, Mandy. I've seen the way you look at him."

"What am I going to do?"

"I think it's time to talk with the bishop," Katie replied sternly.

The sound of horse's hooves and the clatter of a buggy struck Emma's ears.

Who could that be, she wondered. Opening the kitchen door, she stuck her head out and saw a buggy coming down the drive toward the farmhouse. Looking closer, she recognized Tanner's blond hair, light beard, and handsome face.

Has he come to see me? She thought, stepping outside the house and onto the lawn.

"Good morning!" Tanner shouted as he pulled up, climbed out of his buggy, and tied his horse to the hitching post.

"Guten Morgen" replied Emma." Would you like to come in for tea?" she asked, trying to conceal her excitement.

Accepting Emma's offer, Tanner walked up to the porch and followed her inside.

"It was nice to see you at singing last evening," Emma said, pouring a cup of hot tea, carefully handing it to Tanner.

"I was wondering if you might like to go on a picnic with me today."

"I'd love to," replied Emma, taking a sip of her tea, her imagination running wild. "Papa's in town. I'll have to check on my brothers and sisters before I go."

Finishing his tea, Tanner excused himself and went outside. Emma discussed her intentions with her siblings, returned to the house, freshened herself and stepped back outside. Blushing mildly as she climbed into Tanner's one-seat buggy, she leaned against the back board, turned to him, smiled, and sighed deeply.

It was a beautiful day. The southerly wind blew lightly against their faces. Monarch butterflies flitted effortlessly next to the buggy, as if escorting them along the fenced lane to the highway. The soft hum of bees filled the summer air.

It's so good to get away from the farm, Emma thought, as she listened to the sound of the horse's hooves beating a steady rhythm on the road. She smiled as a red tail hawk landed on a fence post in front of them. *Of all the young Amish men interested in dating me, why I am so attracted to this handsome Englishmen?* She wondered.

Tanner pulled off the road, stopped under a grove of trees, stepped to the ground and tethered his horse. Reaching for Emma's hand he helped her down, walked to the back of the buggy, grabbed a blanket and spread it on the grass.

"Tell me about yourself!" Tanner said, opening the paper sack and placing the food on the blanket.

"What would you like to know?"

"Why haven't I seen you at singings?" he queried.

"My mother has been ill. I've been busy tending to her and helping Papa with the farm."

A buggy filled with a group of teens waved as they passed by, shouting, "Guten Tag, Emma Guten Tag, Tanner!"

"Hello!" Tanner shouted back.

Watching as they faded out of sight Tanner placed his hand on Emma's hand and said. "You're the most beautiful girl I've ever seen."

Leaning close, he attempted to kiss her.

"No, you shouldn't," Emma said, pulling back, feeling certain Tanner could hear the sound of her heart pounding against her chest.

"What brought you to the Amish?" Emma asked, putting more space between them.

"I really can't say for sure. Bobby and Sis wanted to visit an Amish settlement and I decided to come along."

"And what do you think of the Amish?"

"I've learned a lot, but I have to admit it's been difficult not having a car, being away from my friends, and living without electricity."

"Do you think you'll ever return to the English world?"

"I don't know."

"Do you have a girl back home?"

"None as pretty as you," he said, looking into Emma's eyes with a sly grin and a subtle wink.

Tanner told Emma about his family, his high school days, and English girls.

Just then a clap of thunder filled the air and the sky began to darken.

"We should go!" Emma exclaimed, rising up quickly, grabbing the remainder of their lunch.

"What's the matter?" Tanner asked.

"There's a storm coming! You better get me home!"

Tanner jerked the blanket off the ground and tossed it into the buggy.

A low, dark bank of clouds began moving their way, followed by incessant sheets of lightning. A hush fell in the air, a steady roll of thunder grew near.

Lifting Emma in the buggy and untying his horse, Tanner jumped into the seat, grabbed the reins, slapped them hard against the horse's broad rump and bolted for the highway.

The sky blackened. The cloud bank came on swiftly. The air became supercharged with electricity. The storm was rapidly catching the buggy. There were only a few seconds between the lighting and the crashing noises of thunder. Through a blinding rush of wind a curtain of rain suddenly descended upon them in stinging sheets.

"Tanner, I'm afraid!" screamed Emma over the roar of the pelting rain, grabbing his arm and holding it as tightly as she could.

"Hold on tight! We'll make it!" he yelled at the top of his voice, snapping the reins harder, pushing the gelding more than he ever had. Speeding down the muddy, pot-holed road they saw other buggies coming from all angles racing to get home, their horses running at break neck speed. Screaming at the top of his voice, Tanner urged his steed on.

Suddenly, as quickly as it had begun, the storm ceased. The ominous rain clouds that'd drenched them fizzled; the rain turned to a light mist. Turning onto the flooded lane to the Yoder farm, the sky became faint with light. A rainbow appeared through the gray-blue sky.

Their clothes soaked, their bodies shivering, they stepped out of the buggy and walked into the house. Standing at the doorway was Amos Yoder.

"Bist du ok?" Amos asked forcefully.

"Ja, Papa" Emma answered, taking a blanket off the couch, handing it to Tanner.

"I'll change into some dry clothes and put on some tea," Emma said, turning toward the stairway.

Shivering as he wrapped the wool blanket tightly around him, Tanner watched Emma climb the stairs to the second floor.

"You should not have taken Emma out in this storm," Amos said, waiting until she was out of sight and sound.

"I'm sorry, Amos. I got her home as quickly as I could. I had no idea a storm was coming."

"Emma's mother is in the hospital and the children need lookin' after. She should've stayed home where she's needed, and not leaving the farm with an Englishman."

"There, I feel better!" Emma exclaimed, skipping down the stairs with a gleeful look on her face. "I'll get that tea now!"

Amos shot a glaring stare at Tanner, turned, and walked out the door.

Emma poured two cups of tea, placed them on the table and removed the blanket from Tanner's shoulders. Sitting down, she looked out the window, her eyes following her father as he stomped across the yard and entered the barn.

"I'll remember this day forever," she said, reaching across the table, touching Tanner's hand.

"So will I," he said.

Reaching up, she brushed Tanner's damp, curly hair off his forehead. Before she could stop herself, she rose, leaned over the table and kissed him softly on the lips.

Hearing the sound of buggy wheels and hoofs on the dirt lane leading to the farm house, she pulled away and looked out of the window.

"It's Mandy," she said, quickly straightening her bonnet and apron.

"Guten Tag!" she said, opening the kitchen door, watching Mandy tie her horse to the post.

"Guten Tag," Mandy replied.

"How are you?" Emma asked.

"Good, thank you," Mandy replied, walking briskly past Emma, into the kitchen.

"Hello Tanner. How are you?" Mandy asked, looking at him through squinted, piercing eyes.

"Still a little wet," Tanner replied sheepishly.

"Petie said he saw the two of you earlier and wondered if you got caught in that terrible thunderstorm."

"Would you like some tea?" Emma asked, pouring a cup.

"Danke," Mandy replied, sitting down, her eyes fixed steadfastly on Tanner.

"Tanner stopped by and asked if I'd like to go on a picnic with him. The storm came up so quickly, we wondered if we were going to make it home in one piece," Emma said, watching as Tanner fidgeted in his chair.

"I really should be going," Tanner said, sensing the increasing tension in the air.

"I'll walk you outside," Emma said, following him out the screen door.

"Will I see you again?" she asked, reaching for his hand as he stepped into his buggy.

"Soon," he answered, bending over, looking into her eyes, remembering their stolen kiss.

Driving home that afternoon, Tanner's mind wandered. What was he going to do? Had his feelings for Mandy been replaced by Emma's beauty and mysterious charm? The mere thought of Emma caused his pulse to quicken.

Mandy pinched her cheeks to add color to her face, brushed on some light mascara, put on her best dress and apron and slipped quietly out the back door. Sitting in his rocker in the front room, Jacob watched as she pulled away in the buggy and wondered how much longer he could allow this to go on. Looking out through the bedroom window,

Katie knew that soon, and very soon, this situation would come to the attention of the bishop, if it hadn't already.

Mandy smiled to herself as the sound of crickets and a hoot owl filled the night air. She was excited about seeing Tanner again. It'd been a few weeks since she'd seen him at Emma's house and she wanted this night to be special. Rounding a corner, she saw him standing alongside the lane, looking handsome in his freshly ironed clothes.

"Guten Abend!" Mandy said, getting out of her buggy.

"Good evening to you!" Tanner replied, reaching for her hand.

Helping Mandy into his buggy, Tanner tied her sorrel mare to its rear wheel.

Stepping back into his buggy, he sat down next to her. Her face seemed to radiate in the fullness of the moon. Her full lips and beautiful long, graceful neck struck him as it had the first time he'd seen her.

"Do you like Emma?" Mandy asked abruptly.

"Why do you ask?" Tanner replied, trying to appear indifferent.

"I saw the way you looked at her at singing and the way she looked at you at her house."

"Aw, it's nothing," Tanner said. "You're my gal, aren't you?"

"I thought I was."

"Come here," he said, pulling her near, trying to kiss her.

"No, Tanner. You must choose between Emma and me," she said, pressing her hands firmly against his chest. "Amish girls are not allowed to date more than one young man at a time. In our way, when a young man seeks permission to court a girl, it is expected that the courtship will likely end in marriage as he will make his decision to court only after great thoughts and prayer."

Tanner backed away, hearing the jingling sound of a harness and voices coming toward them.

"Hello!" a voice cried out. "Wer ist das?"

"It's me!" Tanner yelled, jumping down from his buggy.

"Is that Mandy with you?"

"Yes."

Petie and his date, Anna, stopped next to Tanner's buggy.

"Did you'ns hear about Fannie Yoder?" Petie asked Mandy.

"No. Is something wrong!?"

"She came home this afternoon. The doctors said there was nothing more they could do for her."

"Dear God. Her poor family." Mandy replied.

"It looks like you two want to be alone. We'll be seeing ya!" Petie said, snapping the reins and driving away.

"I have to go," Mandy said, climbing down from Tanner's buggy.

Her thoughts of Tanner had to be put aside. Although her biggest rival for Tanner's attention, Emma had been her friend since childhood and she knew it was only right to focus her thoughts on her friend's pain and the impending tragedy that would soon befall her family.

"I really need to see Tanner," Emma thought to herself with a twang of guilt, remembering the picnic, the storm, and their kiss, as she tucked her mother in bed and returned to her bedroom. Looking through her open window, she wondered when she would see him again.

Just then a bright light flashed through the dark from below and into her room. Startled, she jumped back and out of sight. The light flashed again, then went off.

"Emma!" a voice called out softly.

"Is that you Tanner?"

"Yes."

"Come outside!"

Slipping a shawl over her shoulders, Emma tiptoed down the stairs and walked outside.

"I've missed you," Tanner said quietly.

"I've missed you too."

"How is your mother?"

"She's in a lot of pain."

"I'm so sorry."

"Thank you. We're very concerned about her."

"Papa says I'm not to see you again. He says you'll return to the English one day and he doesn't want to see you hurt me."

Emma was aware her father had talked to the bishop about the two of them seeing each other and that Jacob Beiler had also visited with the bishop about Mandy dating Tanner.

A light came on in the house.

"I must go," Emma whispered firmly, stepping away, running toward the house.

Tanner hadn't spoken to Mandy in weeks. She'd moved into John and Rebecca Schwartz's farmhouse and had not attended church or singings.

Rebecca had recently given birth to their eighth child, was not doing well, and had asked Mandy to help with the children and the chores.

Writing a note asking Mandy to meet him, Tanner gave it to a friend and asked him to deliver it to her. A few weeks passed and he'd still not heard anything. Deciding to ask her himself, he drove his buggy to the Schwartz house.

Seeing him turning into the lane, Mandy walked out to meet him; a wave of heat and tension coming over her with each step she took.

"You shouldn't be here, Tanner," she said pointedly.

"But I need to talk to you!"

"My father has forbidden me to see you again. Please go."

"But I---"

"Go now, please."

Turning his buggy around, Tanner headed for our farm.

"I don't know what to do, Sis," Tanner said, placing his face in his hands, his body trembling uncontrollably.

"What's wrong?" Shelly asked.

"Amos won't let me see Emma, and Jacob told Mandy to stay away from me. How did I get myself into this?"

"I don't know, Tanner. The question now is ...how you're going to get yourself out of it."

Emma looked out of the front room window and saw Tanner's buggy coming toward the farmhouse. She'd sent word that she wanted to see him and was expecting his arrival.

"Hello, Tanner," she said, watching as he stepped down from his buggy.

"Hello."

"The bishop told Papa I can't see you again," Emma said, through tearful eyes. "Go now, please, before I get into more trouble. Papa will be home soon, and will be angry if you're here when he arrives."

Stumbling back to his buggy, feeling like he'd been punched in the stomach, Tanner pulled himself up to the seat, took the reins in his hands and left for Samuel's farm. He'd spoken to Samuel about his feelings for Mandy and Emma, his concern about what the community thought of him, and about what he should do.

Concerned about the influence Tanner had on Mandy and Emma, as well as the lives of their families, Samuel had made it a point to council him, keeping a close eye on the escalating situation.

"Hello Tanner! It's nice to see you again," Samuel said, opening the door, inviting him into his home.

Samuel had also visited with the bishop about this predicament and shared with him that he disapproved of Tanner dating the young maidens in this community. Feeling no good could come from it, he'd urged the bishop to put a stop to it as soon as possible.

"Please have a seat. I'll get us some tea," Samuel said, walking into the kitchen.

"So, my young friend, I understand you've gotten yourself into a bit of a snag," Samuel said, handing Tanner a cup.

"I guess you've heard that Jacob Beiler and Amos Yoder have told Mandy and Emma they cannot see me again. I don't know what to do Samuel."

"Do you care for these girls?"

"I do. That's what makes it so difficult," Tanner said, rubbing his forehead in anguish, looking out through the curtained window.

Samuel had heard about similar situations in large Amish communities in Ohio, Indiana and Pennsylvania but never suspected something like this would occur in their small, secluded Missouri settlement.

"What are your plans for the future?

"I had intended to go to college last year in Oklahoma City, but when Sis and Bobby moved here, I decided to put it off."

"Can you still go?"

"Yes, but---"

"Seems to me you have some serious consideration to give to this situation," Samuel said, getting up to replenish their tea.

"I'd think that a young man in the English world, without proper education, would be doomed to a life of hard labor. Is that what you want for yourself, Tanner?" Samuel said, filling their cups, sitting back down.

Tanner pondered the question and reflected on the plans he'd made before coming to the Amish settlement; plans to go to college, fall in love, get married, have children and enjoy a successful career. It seemed so simple then, and so very complicated now. How could he leave his Amish friends? What about his feelings for Mandy and Emma?

"If you remain in the Amish settlement and wish to become a church member, you must be baptized. Have you given much thought to this?"

"I have."

"Are you ready to make such a commitment?"

"I don't know, I just don't know...now."

A roll of thunder struck the still, heavy air; a storm was developing to the west.

"You have found yourself in a difficult position Tanner. I advise you to take some time to pray about this and do what you feel God is leading you to do. I wish you the best and will support you in whatever decision you make."

"Thank you, Samuel. I appreciate you and will always remember you."

Rising from his chair, Tanner walked to the door, removed his hat from the hook, placed it on his head, looked circumspectly around the room as if attempting to memorize its contents, turned and shook Samuel's hand.

"Gott sei mit Euch," Samuel said, wrapping his feeble hands around Tanner's hand.

"Sir?" Tanner questioned.

"God be with you," Samuel said.

"Hello, Katie, is Mandy home?" Tanner asked, looking through the open front door of the Beiler house. Tanner had left Samuel's farmhouse and headed straight for the Beiler house to see Mandy.

"She's in the barn doing chores," Katie answered, appearing somewhat anxious and evasive.

"Can I see her?"

"No!" Katie said, emphatically.

Katie had never treated Tanner with such coldness. She'd always invited him in. *What have I done to deserve this?* Tanner wondered.

Turning and walking back to his buggy he sat down, snapped the reins, shouted a harsh command, and left.

Sunday night singing was two days away. Tanner knew Mandy would be there and could talk to her.

"Hello, Mandy."

"Hello, Tanner."

"I've missed you," Tanner said, reaching for her hand.

"I've missed you too," Mandy replied, retracting her hand.

"C'mon Mandy, singing's starting," Petie yelled, opening the door to the house.

"Can I take you home tonight?" Tanner asked.

"Yes."

Other than the chiding Tanner received from his friends, Sunday singing went as usual.

"Are you ready to go?" he asked, driving his buggy near Mandy.

"Yes," she replied, sitting in the buggy.

"I can't be gone long. Papa expects me home right away."

"Ok."

Tanner stopped his buggy alongside a field.

"I love you Mandy. I've never felt this kind of love for a girl before."

"I love you too Tanner. I think I loved you the first time I saw you," she replied, turning her face, wiping away a tear.

"What are we going to do?"

"I guess it's up to you, Tanner."

"I miss my family. I miss my friends, I miss all the things we used to do together."

"Maybe you should go back to Oklahoma City and see if it's the same as you remember it."

"Do you think that's what I should do?"

"Yes, I do."

"But I'll miss you!"

"We can write each other," she said, pushing Tanner's hat back on his head, looking into his eyes.

"I'm not very good at writing," Tanner said sheepishly, laughing through his tears.

"That's ok. I'll write for both of us."

"You would do that…"

"Yes…"

"I feel better now," he said, taking a deep breath and letting it out.

"Me too," Mandy said, smiling.

"I guess I'd better get you home."

Silence fell as they drove slowly to the Beiler farmhouse, each wondering what the other was thinking.

"I suppose I'll be leaving soon," Tanner said, helping Mandy down from the buggy, wrapping his arms around her waist.

"You'll write then?" Mandy said.

"I will, I promise."

"Ich liebe dich," Mandy said, looking up into his eyes, knowing she'd never see him again.

"I love you too," Tanner said, kissing her softly, then turning away and climbing back into his buggy.

"Good Bye, Mandy," Tanner whispered under his breath, as he watched her open the front door of the farmhouse.

"Good Bye, Tanner," Mandy wept, looking out through her bedroom window, watching his buggy leave their farm for the last time.

15

Passing of a Loved One

Fall 1971

Tanner rose from bed early one cool, brisk, morning a few days after saying good-bye to Mandy, climbed into his buggy and traveled door to door throughout the settlement, saying good-bye to his Amish family. Returning to our farm later that morning, he wept as Shelly packed a bag of sandwiches, placed it in his hand and hugged him.

Mandy's goodbye had been almost prophetic. The uncertainty of what the future held for him in the Amish community, coupled with his desire to reconnect with his English friends left Tanner with little choice but to pack his bag and hitchhike back to Oklahoma City.

Pleading with him to stay, Dakota ran into Shelly's arms, screaming, "Please don't go! Please don't leave us Tanner," as Tanner walked slowly through the front door, down the steps, across the lawn, and onto the dirt road.

We watched, standing on the porch steps, as he walked out of sight, and out of our lives.

The long, hot, sultry days and warm nights filled with starlit skies, sounds of crickets chirping and frogs croaking were over. Taking their place were cool, crisp mornings and killing frosts. Once-green leaves now turned orange, yellow, and red, drifted freely and effortlessly through the air, landing gently on the frigid ground. Trails of pale, bluish-gray smoke swirled from rooftop chimneys into the silent night. For the Amish, the time of harvest and coming together was near. For nature, it was a time for sowing and scattering.

Work with Eli had not been as plentiful as the previous summer. I hadn't been able to set aside as much money for the winter as I had hoped. Shelly and Katie were busy canning and storing food for the upcoming winter months. Jacob and I would soon butcher our feeder pigs and the steer Eli had given me. It'd been a rough year for many Amish families. We were in for a long, hard winter.

Jacob stopped by one evening in late October, said that my mother had called and left a message for me to contact her as quickly as possible. Getting up early the next morning, I hurried to Jacob's English neighbor's home and placed a call to see if everything was okay. Weeping, as she answered the phone, mother said Grandpa and Grandma Bolin had been visiting relatives in Arkansas, that grandma had fallen into a coma, and had been taken to a nearby hospital.

"The doctor said she had a brain aneurysm, honey and isn't expected to live much longer. Is there any way you could get down there to see her?"

I told her I'd do what I could and went home to share the news with Shelly. She said she would contact Petie and ask if he'd help with the chores.

Getting up early the next morning, I ate breakfast and packed a large paper sack with clean clothes and personal items. I walked the dirt lane to the state highway, stuck out my thumb, and prayed grandma would be alive when I got there.

A few cars had driven by me when I heard the sound of a horn blowing from behind and an engine racing. Turning around, I saw a hand waving frantically from the driver's side window and a man's voice yelling, "Hurry up! Let's go!"

Opening the door and sitting in the passenger seat I placed my paper bag between my legs and closed the sedan door. The driver was clean-shaven, wore a blue dress suit, pressed white shirt and polished black shoes. He appeared to be in his late forties.

"I'm Rick," he said, sticking out his hand.

"Hi! I'm Bobby! Thanks for the ride!" I replied, shaking his hand.

"Where ya headed?" he asked, peering down at my paper sack, then back at me.

"I'm going to Harrison to see my grandma. She's in the hospital there."

"I'm going through Harrison on my way to Little Rock. I'll drop you off at the hospital."

Turning on his signal, Rick pulled back onto the highway and began humming along with the song playing on the radio. It felt strange to be in a car again, listening to the radio and reading billboards as we sped past them at sixty miles an hour. Accustomed to traveling in a horse-drawn buggy, I felt as though I was in a wind tunnel, blasting through its interior at breakneck speed. I noticed, as we passed other cars, people turning and looking at me, causing me to wonder what they were thinking. Not having seen myself in a mirror for some time, I'd forgotten how much my appearance had changed.

I leaned back in the seat, closed my eyes, and thought of grandma. I knew how much grandpa loved her, and what she meant to him. How would he get along without her?

My mind shifted to my children. I wondered how they were doing, and if they missed me.

I began to feel, watching the world pass by me, as though my life was crashing in on me. Guilt and confusion crept into my mind. *Had I been selfish in leaving my family behind and joining* the *Amish?* I wondered. *What if something happens to one of them and I don't hear about it until it is too late?*

A song came on the radio I'd not heard. I was seized, as I listened to the heartfelt lyrics the singer sang. Chills ran up my spine, neck, and arms. Anxiety filled my very being. I felt like I couldn't breathe.

The singer sang of being lost between two worlds, and not feeling as though he belonged in either one.

Was I, too, lost between two worlds?

"Please help me, God," I cried out from within.

Rick stopped the car an hour later. We got out, stretched our legs, and took a bathroom break. "What's it like being Amish?" he asked, starting the car, putting the transmission into gear.

I told him of my family's decision to join the Amish, and of how our lives had changed since we'd become part of the church and community.

"Do you miss your family?"

"Every minute of every day. That's been the hardest thing, being away from our loved ones."

I fell asleep somewhere between Branson and Harrison, and was dreaming I was in California, playing with my children on the front yard of our home when I felt a hand pushing on my shoulder, and a voice saying, "Wake up Bobby. We're here."

"I hope your grandma gets better!" Rick said, as I opened the door and stepped out of the car.

"Thank you, I hope so too. Thanks again for the ride. God bless you."

I was greeted by stares and whispers as I crossed the sidewalk and walked through the double glass doors of the hospital foyer. Small children, playing on the floor, looked up and ran quickly to their mothers' laps, frightened by my appearance.

"It's okay honey, the Amish man won't hurt you," I heard a mother say to her small child, picking her up, smiling at me.

Scanning the room for familiar faces I heard a "ding," noticed the elevator doors open, and saw Grandpa Bolin walk into the foyer. Smiling, I breathed a sigh of relief, walked over to him and said "Hi, Grandpa!"

"Bobby! Oh my Lord. How did you get here?" he asked, looking tired and haggard.

"I hitch hiked from Missouri. Mother told me about grandma and I wanted to see her."

He told me, as we walked toward the cafeteria, how much he loved me and missed having me in his life. Noticing people staring as we passed through the halls into the cafeteria, I felt uncomfortable, as though I were some kind of sideshow in a carnival.

"Had I been that obvious when I first met Jacob and Katie?" I wondered.

We talked over supper about the events leading up to grandma becoming ill. Where they'd been. Family members they'd seen. Grandpa said grandma was in critical condition, that everyone was praying she'd come out of her coma, but that the doctors were not giving her much of a chance.

"I heard from your momma that you'd taken up with the Amish," he said, tentatively.

I told him that we had, and of how much we enjoyed the Amish people, and living on a farm. He asked if the Amish followed the Bible. I assured him they were Christians, that we were in excellent hands, and of how living the Amish way of life reminded me of his Arkansas farm.

"I'm proud to hear that, son," he said, looking at me through weary eyes. The stress and fear of losing grandma was taking its toll.

"Your momma says you have a farm, raise you own garden, and travel by horse and buggy."

"Yes sir! Every time I hitch up my horse to my buggy, I remember helping you hook up your mules to the wagon and going out to the fields. I'll never forget those days grandpa, as long as I live."

"That means a lot to me, son. You know, you have always been grandpa's boy."

We finished our dinner, took the elevator to grandma's room, opened the door and walked in. Standing next to her bed were several uncles and aunts I'd not seen in years. Startled by my appearance, Uncle Kenny looked at me and said, "Can I help you sir?"

"It's Bobby!" He's come to see his grandma!" Grandpa said loudly.

"Is that you, Bobby?" Aunt Juanita asked, looking me up and down in disbelief.

"Yep. It's me, in the flesh!"

"What've you done to yourself, son?" Uncle Kenny asked, coming over and giving me a bear hug. "I heard you joined some kind of cult. Is that true!"

"No, Shelly and I joined the Old Order Amish," I said, holding on to him as he lifted me off the floor, "and they are *not* a cult."

"Do they believe in the same God that we do?" he asked, motioning for me to sit down.

"Yes they do. We wouldn't be there if they didn't!"

"Well, I heard you had gone off and joined some religious group, but I didn't believe it!"

"You sure are a sight!" Aunt Juanita said, bending over, checking on grandma. "Come here and say hello to your sweet grandma!"

I walked slowly to grandma's bedside. She was lying on her back, perfectly still. The covers were folded neatly across her chest. Her hands were lying by her sides. Reaching down and softly stroking her left hand, I told her how much I loved her and what she meant to me.

Tears began to flow as I remembered her smile, her soft voice, how she loved to sit in her rocker and read the Bible, often times calling me to her side, pointing out a verse, and reading it out loud to me. I remembered seeing her standing in the front pew of grandpa's church, singing and softly patting her hand against her Bible as the choir sang her favorite songs.

I don't know how long I stood there, reliving the past in my mind, but the feel of grandpa's hand gently touching my shoulder brought me back to my senses.

"We better go now, son," he said, tugging on my sleeve.

That was the last time I saw grandma. She became well enough for grandpa to take her back to California and died shortly after. She was buried in Arkansas, where grandpa was also buried years later.

I went downstairs and visited with family members before going to the motel room with grandpa. We sat up into the night, reminiscing about old days and how times had changed. He told me again how proud he was that I was following the Lord and how much he missed me. He said if I was happy, and living a Christian life, that was all that mattered to him.

We got up the next morning and had breakfast together. I told him I needed to get back to the farm. He told me how much he appreciated me coming to see grandma and offered to buy me a bus ticket home. I thanked him and said I'd make it home okay.

I picked up a ride from a trucker outside Harrison. After telling him about grandma, he turned up his radio and said, "I'll leave you alone. You'd probably like some time to yourself."

Opening the gate to the farm house, I walked across the lawn to the front door and went inside. Shelly was singing a hymn and putting dishes away in the kitchen cabinets. I walked across the front room into the kitchen, wrapped my arms around her and told her how happy I was to be home.

"We're happy you're home safely. You must be hungry. Sit down, I'll get you some food."

Heating fried chicken, mashed potatoes, and brown gravy they'd had the previous night, she placed them on the table.

"How long did you have to walk before you got a ride?" she asked, pulling my hand away from my face, wiping away a tear.

I told her I'd hitched a ride not long after stepping on the highway that took me to the front door of the hospital and that I'd seen grandpa, grandma and a few of my aunts and uncles.

"How did your grandma look?" she asked, gripping my hand, her eyes fixed on me.

"Bad."

"I'm so sorry, Bobby."

The afternoon slowly rolled into nightfall and the air, which had been clear, filled with a light mist. My mind wandered back to grandpa and grandma's old farmhouse and the many sweet memories we'd made there.

Lying in our feather bed that evening, I kissed Shelly softly on her forehead as she lay sleeping on her untroubled pillow, her hand lying on my chest. A glimmer of light shone through the curtains, projecting a brilliant ray against the bedroom wall. Looking out the window, I could see God's unmoved, eternal lights, and thought of grandma.

16

Lillie Mae

Down the road a piece from our house, on the south side of the lane, lived a petite, well dressed elderly woman named Lillie Mae. Folks around town, and those in the Amish community, simply called her L.M. I met L.M. while coming home from work late one afternoon.

Walking out of her quaint little cottage, past narrow, straight rows of where colorful flowers and a truck patch full of onions, potatoes, corn and beans had flourished the previous summer, she waved her white laced handkerchief daintily above her head.

Dressed in a pretty yellow chiffon dress, her shoulders were partially covered with an elegant knitted white shawl. Finishing off her ensemble were white patent leather shoes, a yellow hat, and white gloves.

I pulled back hard on the reins, slowed the buggy, and stopped at the end of her drive.

"Hello, young man. Could you please come see what's wrong with my television?" she asked, her words flowing in a southern drawl like sweet Tupelo honey from her painted lips, her eyelashes fluttering effortlessly as she spoke. I was instantly captivated by her charm.

Curious as to why a fashionably dressed, venerable English lady would stop me, an Amish man, and ask for help, I replied politely, "I don't know if I can be of any service ma'am."

"Well, I heard you used to be an Englishman and thought you'd know something about my television. Could you please take a look? It won't take but a minute and I'd be forever grateful," she said, moving closer to my buggy.

I looked down to see a comely, genteel, radiant woman, with the most beautiful green eyes and cream colored porcelain skin I'd ever seen. Her eyebrows were plucked perfectly. Her shoulder length, wavy silver hair, and the graceful manner with which she carried herself told me she'd enjoyed a life of luxury.

"It's almost supper time, and I really should be getting home," I said politely. "I'll take a look and see what I can do," pulling Comet to the nearest tree, tying him to a low-lying limb.

"Thank you so much, darlin!" she said, turning and sauntering back down the drive toward her single story cottage, her string purse hanging lazily by her side.

"They say you can tell when a tornado's coming by watching your television screen," she said, walking up the steps to her porch, past a white wooden swing and into the front door of her cottage, "if you turn the television knob to where there's no channel when it's storming and keep a close watch on the screen it will turn green when a tornado comes near."

"You don't say?" I replied, turning on her TV.

"Yes-siree, that's what they say!" she said, smiling widely, coming closer to me as I turned the knob, trying to find a channel.

She has to be eighty years old, I thought to myself. *I wonder if she has family here.*

"There. I think I have it!" I said, seeing a face appear on the television screen.

"Well I do declare! How in the world did you do that sir?"

"Just luck I suppose."

"Could I get you a hot cup of coffee? Ya'll Amish folk do drink coffee don't you? Say, I just baked a coconut cake, and I really hate to eat alone. I'll cut you a slice to go with your coffee!"

"Well…."

"Now, now young man. Your wife has nothing to worry about with me. You just tell her you were with L.M., everyone round these parts knows me. By the way, what's your name?"

"Bobby."

"Well, Bobby, you just git yourself in my kitchen, sit down, make yourself ta' home and tell me all about you and your lovely family!"

Pulling a chair back away from the table, I sat down and began telling her about Shelly, Tanner, Dakota, my family in California, and how we came about joining the Old Order Amish. She poured each of us a cup of hot coffee and showed me pictures of her deceased husband, her children and her grandchildren.

"Would you like to see a picture of me when I was a young woman?" she asked, pushing her chair back, rising and walking into her bedroom.

"I'd love to," I replied, hardly getting the words out of my mouth before she'd returned with a beautifully framed 8x10 picture of herself.

"That picture was taken the day before I was to be married," she said, reaching across the table, placing it in my hands. "Henry was the most handsome, wonderful man I'd ever known. And I was the happiest girl in the world! That was so long ago, yet it seems as though it was just yesterday," she said sighing deeply, casting her eyes away, and blotting them with a handkerchief.

"You were beautiful."

"Thank you, darlin," she said, gently removing the picture from my hands, looking at it wistfully, pressing it to her chest, and returning it to her bedroom.

I took the last sip from my cup, used my fork to gather up the fine crumbs on my plate, wiped my mouth with the pink laced cloth napkin and said, "I really should be going now. My wife is probably wondering what's taking me so long."

"I'll walk you to the door," she said, rising from her chair and placing her frail hand on mine.

"You worked late today!" Shelly said as I walked into the house, removed my boots and hung up my hat.

"I stopped by to help L.M."

"L.M.?"

"Yes, she's the elderly lady that lives down the road on the left hand side. You know, in that pretty little white cottage with the white picket fence, Rhode Island Red chickens and Jersey cow.

"Oh, her! That's her name, L.M.?"

"Yeah, that's what everybody calls her! She wanted me to take look at her television. It wasn't getting any channels."

A few weeks went by. I saw L.M. outside her cottage as I passed by on my way to town, to work, or to help other Amish families with their chores. Hearing Comet trotting down the lane she waved and shouted, "Hey, Bobby! How ya'll doin'?"

I awakened one morning at first light, dressed, washed and dried my face and ran a large tooth comb through my hair. Looking through the kitchen window, I could barely see the silhouette of the large elm tree in the pasture twenty yards away. An unseasonably cold weather front had set in overnight.

Lighting the kerosene lamp, I poured myself a cup of the previous night's cold, dark coffee. Gulping it down I picked up an Amish periodical and slowly turned the pages, waiting for the weather to clear. The dense morning fog brought back memories of the San Joaquin Valley, where damp, cold, wintry days are common. Rising from my chair, I watched as the sun's pallid light filtered through the clouds, slowly illuminating neighboring farm houses, rolling hills and trees.

Coming home from Eli's farm that afternoon I saw her sitting in a swing on her front porch. Looking out over her yard, she appeared to be expecting someone. Bundled in a large fur lined white leather jacket and white leather gloves, her head was covered with a yellow cotton hat. Waving frantically as I grew closer she stopped swinging, stood and walked down the steps to the yard, straddling mud puddles as she continued down the drive.

"Howdy!" she cried out, approaching the buggy, reaching out and softly stroking Comet's nose. Stretching his neck, he took a step closer and nibbled gently at her coat pocket.

"Land sakes, you've got a pretty smart horse! He knows I have something in my pocket!"

Reaching into her coat pocket, she pulled out a shiny red apple and placed it in her open palm. Comet sniffed it, neighed softly, gave it a gentle nudge with his nose and took a bite out of it.

"Say, I've got some Christmas decorations and a few other things I'd like to take down from my attic to go through before Christmas. I hurt my back carrying a bucket of milk to the house yesterday. Ol' Bess gave more than she usually does and it was full to the brim! Could you help me with them?"

"I'd be happy to."

"Is Saturday morning okay?"

"Sounds good! I'll see you after chores!"

Shelly and I had decided we would not decorate for Christmas. Our hearts and minds were far away, with our families. The pain of not being with them at this time of year had brought tears of loneliness, frustration, and sadness. Helping L.M., I reckoned, might help get me out of the doldrums.

Saturday morning arrived. I harnessed Comet and took the short buggy ride to L.M.'s house. Waiting for me in her front porch swing, wrapped in a lovely hand-sewn blanket she'd purchased from an Amish woman in our settlement, she waved as I pulled up and tied off Comet.

"C'mon in and have a cup of coffee, fresh made buttermilk biscuits and sausage gravy!"

Sitting down at the small wooden kitchen table, I leaned forward and wrapped my hands around a warm cup of coffee. L.M. was busy at the stove stirring gravy with a large wooden spoon and watching as the biscuits slowly turned a golden brown.

"Today is Henry's birthday," she said, glancing at me as she turned around. "He would've been 75."

Turning back around, she poured the gravy into a bowl, removed the pan of biscuits from the oven and set them on the table.

"He was killed in an accident a year after we were married. Our families lived in Savannah. Henry's mother and father had a fine three story home with seven bedrooms. His younger brother, Jim, also lived there and worked in the shipyards with him. They worked twelve, sometimes fifteen hours a day. I had a waitress job at Lulu's Diner and worked breakfast, dinner and supper. We hated being away from each other, but were saving money to pay cash for our first home, a home where we could raise a family."

Sitting down across the table from me she bowed her head, blessed the food and began eating.

Enthralled by her story I took a bite of a biscuit covered with hot gravy and set my fork down on the plate.

"I was at work and was taking a break after the breakfast rush when a police officer walked through the door and asked for me. The manager told him I was in the back room. Overhearing their conversation, I stood up and straightened my clothes to greet him. The officer introduced himself, and told me that Henry had been killed in an accident at work. He said Henry had been moving material under a crane, the crane had lost its load, and Henry had been crushed by the weight. He said there was nothing anyone could do to save him. The officer's words began to sound as though they were coming from a tunnel. The next thing I knew he was picking me up off the floor and setting me in a chair at the table. Staying long enough to make sure I was alright, he told me to contact him if there was anything he could do."

"I'm so sorry," I said, gently touching her hand "We'd better get started."

I spent the rest of the morning bringing boxes down from her attic. Opening and sorting the contents L.M. came across pictures she and Henry had taken before they were married and during their first year together. With each picture came tears, as she reminisced about the past.

"Is there anything I can do?" I asked.

"No, darlin. I'll be ok."

A month went by. Seeing no lights in her home, and no activity outside as I passed by late one afternoon I stopped to check on her. As I reached to knock on the front door I was greeted by an English lady.

"L.M. is not here. She took a bus out of Springfield to visit her family in the South."

The bishop's message that Sunday about family had been particularly moving. Contemplating his words, I couldn't help but wonder how L.M. was doing. I missed seeing her, hearing her voice.

Turning off the road and pulling into our drive, I noticed something white stuck to our front door. Intrigued, I stopped, let Shelly and Dakota out of the buggy, drove Comet to the barn, put him away, and hurried back to the house.

"L.M. left a note on our door." Shelly said, handing a folded piece of paper to me as I walked into the house. "What does it say?" she asked, walking back to the kitchen.

I unfolded the paper and began to read. "She's back home, and would like to have us over next Saturday afternoon for hot chocolate and cookies."

"Well, look at you, darlin! All dressed up in your little black hat, suspenders, and polished shoes. Sakes, alive! You look just like your daddy!" Lillie Mae said, seeing Shelly and Dakota for the first time, turning on her southern charm, looking as though she'd stepped out of a beauty parlor.

"What's your name, honey?"

"Dakota."

"Well, Dakota, I'm Lillie Mae. I must say I'm very pleased to meet such a handsome young man. And this pretty lady standing next to you must be your momma."

"Yes Ma'am!"

"Hello. I'm Bobby's wife, Shelly."

"I'm pleased to meet you, honey. Ya'll come in out of the cold, sit down on the couch and make yourselves ta' home."

Sashaying through the living room, she left us and walked into the kitchen.

A large table sat on the living room floor. On it sat a number of opened cardboard boxes filled with Christmas decorations. An undecorated seven foot Christmas tree stood on its pedestal in front of the bay window.

"I thought ya'll might like to help me decorate my living room. Decorating for Christmas always puts me in a cheerful mood," she said, looking through the doorway separating the living room and kitchen, filling the mugs with hot chocolate.

"Would you like some help?" Shelly asked.

"Yes, darlin'! That's awfully sweet of you to ask. Do you like lemon cookies, Dakota?" asked L.M., sitting down in a large tufted white fabric chair across from us.

"Yes Ma'am."

"Oh, honey, please call me L.M.!"

"Yes Ma'am."

"Bobby told me quite a bit about you, Shelly. I'll bet it was difficult making the transition to the Amish life."

"It took some time, and a lot of praying," Shelly replied.

"I can only imagine. Giving up electricity, a washer, dryer, running water, and having to take a horse and buggy to town to do you're shopping! It would take a very strong woman to make those kinds of sacrifices. What did your family think of your decision to join the Amish?"

"They were concerned at first because they thought I'd joined a cult. But in time they realized the Amish followed Jesus, as they do."

"Should we get started?" I asked, noticing Shelly had begun to squirm in her seat.

I set my empty cup on the coffee table, rose, stretched, and walked towards the open boxes.

Asking Dakota if he'd like to help her, L.M. took one last sip and placed her cup on an end table.

Shadowing her every step, Dakota removed shiny glass tree ornaments from the boxes and handed them to L.M. Giggling as she told him what a big help he was, he took extra care not to drop one. Shelly and I followed with icicles, garland and lights. I placed a beautifully dressed white angel on the top of the tree. L.M. handed me a wreath she'd brought back from Savannah and asked me to hang it on the outside of the front door.

I watched as Dakota skipped around the room, smiling and admiring the decorations we'd put up. Seeing the joy and excitement in his eyes I couldn't help but wonder if Shelly and I had made a bad decision about not decorating.

"I made a pot of chili and a gallon jar of sweet tea last evening. Ya'll relax and I'll cut the corn bread."

Sitting back, I reclined against the back of the soft couch. I'd not slept well the night before. Shelly reached over and gently stroked my hair. Watching from the kitchen, Dakota ran into the living room, jumped on the couch between us, leaned back, placed his left hand on Shelly's thigh, his right hand on my thigh, sighed heavily, looked up at us and smiled. L.M. called us to the table. We joined hands as she offered a prayer.

L.M. talked about her family during dinner, saying she'd become close to Jim, Henry's brother after Henry's accident. She said he'd taken her under his wing, saw to it that she was taken care of, and that even though she grew to love him, she always wondered what life would've been like with Henry.

"Jim and I had four children together. That's their pictures hanging on the wall. Jim died ten years ago. He came home from work one day, sat down in his chair, leaned forward to untie his shoes, and fell face down on the floor.

The doctor said it was cardiac arrest. A cousin of mine, living in Springfield asked me to visit her after his death. I came out, bought this farm, and am still here!"

We finished supper. I picked up Dakota, took him to the couch and covered him. He'd fallen asleep in his chair. Shelly helped L.M. in the kitchen.

"The next morning, sitting at our kitchen table, recalling the pleasure we three had shared decorating L.M.'s cottage I said to Shelly," I think we should put up our Christmas decorations today."

"I think so too," she said, with a smile.

17

To Every Season

Wild Canadian geese flew south as the ancient maple and oak trees lost their brilliant colors and became barren. Cool, brisk, fall days faded into cold, dark, biting wintry months. Roses, lilies, and other plants tucked themselves away securely until warm breezes and sunny days would once again announce their rebirth. As I had done the previous winter, I helped fill silos, fed, and butchered animals and looked after farms for Amish families visiting their kinfolk in Indiana. We attended an Amish wedding in December.

Amish weddings are a detailed and painstaking undertaking and not the result of a capricious affair. Fancy printed wedding announcements are shunned. Plain post cards instead are sent to family members living far away. Wedding clothing is the same attire worn to church services. Alcoholic beverages are verboten.

Celebrations are exhaustive because much is expected from the couple regarding community compliance, responsibility and becoming a part of the settlement. Dowries are homemade items and crafts provided by families. Dishes, lamps, blankets, bed spreads, towels, clocks, household items, tools and farm equipment are given to the newlywed couple as presents. The parents of the couple provide furniture, farm animals, quilts and comforters. Competition as to who spent the most money on gifts, or gave the most glamorous present is considered prideful and boisterous.

Marriage is not only seen as a nexus between two people, but as a bond with the community as well, as it strengthens, solidifies and furthers their way of life. The Amish believe a man and woman become "one flesh," and as such are married for life. Separation is unheard of. The word "divorce" is not found in their vocabulary.

The wedding day is a celebration enjoyed by both the young and the elderly. Before the festivities begin, the bride and groom are taken to a council room where they're provided instructions regarding marital duties.

Outside the room the assembly sings wedding hymns. Returning to the assembly the couple sits in the front row as the minister delivers his sermon on marriages from the Old Testament.

After a long sermon, the couple is asked to come forward, exchange their vows and answer a few questions. The minister places his hand on their joined hands and utters a blessing on them. The couple join their right hands and the Bishop pronounces them husband and wife.

A driver takes the married couple to the bride's home for the wedding dinner. Guests park their buggies, visit and are seated at tables filled with duck, chicken, ham, potatoes, gravy, salad and desserts of all kinds.

Immediately after dinner folks begin to sing upbeat hymns, lasting until late in the afternoon, when a full supper is set on the large tables. Hymns are sung during the meal and until late that evening. Finishing their supper, young people chase each other to the barn and play games until after midnight. The newly wedded couple spend the night at the home of the bride. There is no honeymoon scheduled.

I became ill shortly after the wedding with a severe kidney infection that resisted every drug my doctor prescribed. The Old Order Amish do not carry commercial health insurance, are much less likely to seek medical care, and typically cover medical expenses from contributions from the community.

I'd trained with some of the top ranked professional and amateur boxers in the world in my mid-late teens. Fighting in a "smoker" one

Saturday night, an errant punch to my right kidney ruptured it, causing it to be removed. Becoming increasingly concerned about the condition of my remaining kidney, my doctor advised me to see a specialist.

We struggled through the winter months, fighting the bitter cold as freezing temperatures numbed our ears, noses, hands, and feet. After what seemed to be an eternity of breaking ice to get water for the animals, walking to the outhouse through freezing, foggy mornings and trying to stay warm in a house with very little insulation, spring finally arrived--and with it, hope.

We moved from the Johnson farmhouse into a one story home across the state highway. My kidney infection had cleared up and we looked forward to another season. Eli contacted me in May, saying he had work installing cabinets in two English homes. Shelly became pregnant in February, had difficulty regulating her blood pressure and began suffering from hypertension. My doctor advised me, after another bout with kidney infection, to see a specialist in Oklahoma City.

Tanner, now living in Oklahoma City, called us on our English neighbor's phone often, keeping us up to date on what was going on in his life. Attending college part time and working full time, he said he didn't have the time for a girlfriend, that he was still in love with Mandy, and that he missed us. It wasn't the same with him gone. Dakota missed him terribly, asked about him every day, and cried himself to sleep for weeks after he left.

The house we'd rented was several miles away from the closest Amish family and was surrounded by English homes. As the months passed we began to feel less a part of the Amish community, almost as if we were living in separate worlds. Other than church every two weeks, we saw very little of Jacob and Katie, and even then the relationship seemed strained.

I received a letter from Mother saying she and Dad would be driving up from Tennessee to see us. She'd decided not to reveal our life style to Dad, figuring we would not stay long enough with the Amish to bother him with the information.

Hearing them pull up and getting out of their Volkswagen Beetle I opened the front door of the house, stepped out on the porch and shouted, "Guten Tag!"

Mother looked up, saw me dressed in black, with a full beard and my hair cropped and broke into tears. Dad stood next to the car, holding the door handle in his hand, wondering if they'd come to the wrong house.

"Is that you, Bobby?" he asked.

"Yes."

"What in the--" he replied, halting his words half way through the sentence.

Quickly closing her door, Mother rushed up the stairs, onto the front porch.

"He'll be okay, honey. Just give him some time," she whispered in my ear, wrapping her arms tightly around me.

Things settled down after a few days. We took Mother and Dad to meet some of our Amish family. Dad took over the reins of the buggy on several occasions, sitting up straight, looking around proudly as we drove through the countryside.

A week came and passed. We stayed up late catching up on family affairs, laughing, crying, and remembering old times.

I was torn, watching as their light blue Volkswagen pulled away that Sunday morning. A part of me was happy they'd come, yet another part, deep within my being, screamed for them to turn the car around and come back.

The English world I'd left suddenly came crashing back into my mind. And now, as they pulled out of sight, I yearned to see my children in California, to hold them and tell them how much I loved and missed them.

Standing in the middle of the dirt lane, trying to catch one last image of them, I felt as though I was sinking, and the deeper I sank, the fainter my screams for help became, until they faded into echoes I alone could hear.

Shelly continued to experience problems with her pregnancy. Due to deliver in November, she talked to her aunt in Oklahoma City and decided to see a specialist there. Hiring an English neighbor to take them to the bus station, she and Dakota left mid-September.

I tried to keep busy while they were away. Working with Eli helped, but the emptiness was unbearable. As the weeks passed, and darker days drew near, missing my family became a weight I could not bear. I began to question what I was doing, why I came, why I was there, where I belonged. My life was in a constant state of turmoil.

Hitching up Comet to the buggy one morning I'd made plans to meet Eli at a job site. As I was preparing to step up into the buggy a cat ran out of the barn and under Comet's legs, causing him to bolt and run. Realizing what'd happened, I grabbed the reins and screamed for him to stop but it was too late. Knocked down by the left rear wheel, I landed on my face. Rising to my feet, I gasped as Comet raced down the dirt road at full gallop, turning and swerving at breakneck speed.

"Whoa! Comet! Whoa!" I screamed, watching in horror as the buggy wheels hit a deep pothole. Bouncing high in the air, the buggy flipped sideways and crashed to the earth, shattering into broken pieces.

As it fell, a sharp piece of wood struck Comet's rear leg, causing him to limp and bleed profusely. Unable to run, I limped slowly down the lane, crying hopelessly in despair. Taking hold of the reins, I led him slowly back to the farm.

The damage to his leg was irreparable. He had to be put down that evening. My buggy was beyond repair. Sick, downtrodden, broke, and missing my family, I was at my wit's end.

It was that day that I decided to leave the Missouri Amish and return to Oklahoma City. Lying in bed that evening, I couldn't help but think of the irony of the situation. A picture of an Amish buggy that'd been in an accident was what brought my family to the Amish settlement, and an accident with my buggy was what prompted the end to our time there.

Was this a life lesson for me to learn? Was it all meant to be? Should we have never come to the Amish settlement? I guess I'll never know the answers to those questions.

Wiping tears away from my eyes, I embraced my Amish family and told them goodbye. It was the hardest thing I've ever had to do.

18

Return to the English Way

Shelly delivered a healthy daughter in November. I found a job working as a wrangler at a large quarter horse ranch outside of Oklahoma City. Advising the ranch manager I needed more help, I convinced him to hire Tanner to feed stock and clean stalls.

Hearing about an upcoming boxing program in Oklahoma City, I contacted the promoter and soon began teaching boxing in the evenings, judging bouts, and working corners.

The fighting and bickering Shelly and I thought we'd left in our past resumed almost as if it had never ceased. Tanner and Dakota decided they would like to give boxing a try. Under my guidance, Tanner enjoyed some success fighting on local amateur boxing cards. Dakota went on to win numerous state championships on the west coast, Alaska and Canada. Shelly became pregnant again and gave birth to a son in 1974.

It'd been some time since I'd ridden a horse but working ten hours a day on the back of the Palomino mare I'd been assigned quickly got me back into shape. The ranch manager, noticing how I worked with the other men, promoted me to head up the wrangling crew. It was on a roundup that I came close to losing my leg, and possibly my life.

Rustling up the cattle from a back pasture on the ranch, a group of riders and I were heading them into large holding pens to be wormed and receive medical treatment. As I rode into the holding pen and along the fence, I watched as they worked the enormous Texas longhorns, notorious for being independent, unpredictable, and downright mean. With horn spans of up to sixty eight inches, they've been known to gore cowboys, sometimes killing them.

I pulled back on the reins, stopped the mare, relaxed in my saddle, and watched as a large bull refused to be coerced into a corral. A battle of wills was going on between him and the young wrangler, and the bull was winning. Seeing the bull outsmart the cowboy time and again, I decided the wrangler could use a little help. Whistling loudly, waving my arms in the air, I yelled at him to back off, gave the palomino mare a sharp jab in her ribs with both spurs and headed her towards the corral, a short thirty yards away. She lunged forward and quickly broke into a full gallop.

Observing us coming towards him, the angry bull spun, shook his head violently side to side, pawed the dirt, and snorted loudly. He turned, leapt forward, and began running toward us, pitching his head side to side throwing snot and bellowing as he grew near.

Galloping towards the bull, now headed straight for us, I jerked the reins hard to the right to avoid a collision. The quarter horse mare, feeling the leather reins against her neck, dug her hooves into the dirt and cut sharply. Before I knew it the bull was upon us, lunging toward the mare. She turned her head towards the bull, her body quivering under me, as she anticipated the pain from the thrust of his horn, her large, bloodshot eyes filled with fear.

Seeing the bull dip his head to attack, I grabbed the saddle horn for support, raised my left leg and watched as he plunged his long, sharp horn deep into the mare's belly. Critically injured, she grunted loudly, fell to her knees, and threw me over her head, where I rolled head over heels into the dirt. Seeing the bull charging at me, I leaped to my feet, ran as fast as I could to the fence, and climbed to the top rail--my body shaking out of control.

Running to the fence where I was sitting, the bull snorted and let out a blood curdling sound. Looking at me through eyes that would scare Satan himself, he turned, walked away slowly, stopped, looked back at me, and trotted away, taunting me to step down from the fence.

I had difficulty sleeping that evening. Tossing and turning, throwing the covers off me, then pulling them back up, I played the scene over and over in my head. When sleep did arrive, my dreams were filled with the sound of pounding hooves, heavy breathing, and the sight of the bull's angry eyes as he bore his horn into the frightened mare's body. Each time I awoke I could hear the pitiful sound she made as she collapsed and fell to the earth, blood pouring from the huge gape in her side, mouth and nostrils.

"Bobby, come here quick!" Tanner shouted the next morning, as I parked my car next to the ranch barn and opened the door. "The mare's dead and you won't believe it. She was pregnant!"

"What? No!"

"Yes, I'm telling you the truth. They found out when the doctor checked her."

Walking quickly alongside him, reliving the previous day's events again, we came to the barn door, opened it and saw a group of men standing together. Peering over the ranch manager's shoulder, I saw the Palomino mare lying on the concrete floor.

"They did all they could to save her. She died early this morning," he said, looking somberly at me.

I went about the day, performing my duties, but things were never the same. A few months later the owner, going through difficult economic times, sold off many of his cattle and let me go, leaving me jobless.

Hearing of our situation through family members, Shelly's cousin, Andy, called to tell her there was work in Oregon. With the few dollars we had left in our pockets, and a promise to pay back the money we borrowed from her relatives, we packed our car and left for Salem.

Hitting the streets as soon as we arrived, I found full time employment working the swing-shift at the State Juvenile Correctional System.

Determined to do something with my life I began taking business, computer, and psychology courses at the local community college during the day, and working as a security officer between classes. Maintaining this hectic schedule helped to keep my mind off my Amish family, and the way of life I'd left behind.

Samuel and David wrote often, keeping me apprised of what was happening in the Amish community. My thoughts continued to drift back to my family there, and the Amish lifestyle. There were times when I considered returning, but knew I couldn't live that far away from family again.

Finding it equally difficult to make the transition from the Amish to the English life, Shelly called me several times a day at work and at school, crying, and asking me what she was supposed to do with herself. I felt bad about the amount of time I had to spend away from her and the children, but knew if I did not continue with my job and education, we would be doomed to a life of poverty.

Coming home from work one evening I pulled into the driveway, got out of my car, opened the front door of the house and walked into an empty living room. Stunned, I screamed out, "Shelly, where are you?"

Darting in and out of the kitchen, bathroom, and bedrooms, I quickly discovered the entire house was empty. The realization of what'd happened suddenly hit me. She'd left and taken our furniture and the children with her. Staring at the bare walls, windows, and empty closets, I fell to my knees and burst into tears.

"Why, Shelly, why?" I cried out.

Gathering my thoughts, I rose, closed our bedroom door, sat in the middle of the unoccupied front room and buried my face in my hands. Sobbing, I curled into a fetal position and pleaded to God to give me an answer as to why my family had been taken from me. A gentle rain fell outside. The sound of the drops running off the roof and into the rain gutter lulled me to sleep.

Awakening the next morning to the silence and the starkness of what had become our home I sat up and lifted my stiff, sore body off the carpet. Walking to the kitchen counter I picked up the telephone and dialed Andy's phone number. We'd become close friends, going to church together and sharing our love for Christian music. I knew he could provide information about my family's whereabouts.

"Shelly called me after you left for work yesterday afternoon, Bobby. She told me she was going to California, and asked if I would help load the truck she'd rented before you returned home from work."

"How could she do this to me, Andy?" I asked, startled by his words.

"She's been planning it for weeks. She asked me not to tell you."

I thanked him, hung up the phone, walked outside, got into my car and headed to the coastal town of Oceanside. I couldn't help but remember, as I drove westward through the small villages along the way, the good times my family and I had had there, picnicking and playing on the beach, and walking through the cave at Maxwell Point.

Arriving at Oceanside I parked my car, opened the door, and walked a short trail to the beach. The rain had turned into a soft drizzle. A cool wind blew in my face. Turning up my collar, I continued north to the cave where I hoped to find solace, but instead found myself hearing my children's laughter, and seeing them running and laughing as they raced through the cave and into the oncoming waves on the far side.

Grief-stricken, I stumbled through the next three months, trying to focus on my job, and spending my days in class and studying. Attempts to contact Shelly failed. Coming to the realization that I could not go on without her and our children, I took a week off work and drove south to California.

I found Shelly after several phone calls and pleaded with her to return to Oregon with me, telling her I needed her and the children back in my life. A week later, after numerous attempts to convince her to come home, I left alone and returned to the room in Salem I'd rented.

Feeling as though Andy had betrayed me, and having no family support in Oregon, I quit my job and flew to Fairbanks, Alaska to stay with family, where I quickly found a job in the facilities division of the Fairbanks North Star Borough School District.

It wasn't long before Shelly began calling and asking how I was doing, and if I missed her and the children. I told her I was doing the best I could under the circumstances and that I was trying to move on with my life. She told me she'd been working as a cocktail waitress, had become pregnant, and wanted to try to put our marriage back together. Packing the car, she and the children left a few weeks later and drove to Fairbanks.

We worked at trying to keep our marriage together, but the love we once had for each other had faded and been replaced with apathy, uncertainty, and distrust. Sadly, our marriage ended in divorce.

Tanner left Oklahoma City, returned to Fresno, married an old high school flame and went to work in the construction business. We call each other often, talk about the "Amish days," and have agreed to return to Missouri to visit our family there one day.

Dakota grew up sharing his time between his mother and me after the divorce. Married and divorced now, he has two boys in their early twenties.

My new wife, Pat, and I returned to the Amish settlement in 2007. Picking up David and Suzie, we drove past Amos' and Samuel's farm houses and pulled into Eli's drive. His wife told us we'd just missed him, said she would tell him we had stopped by, and asked us to come back the next time we were in Missouri.

Backing out of Eli's drive, I was drawn to the old farmhouse where Shelly and I had lived. Memories flooded my mind as I peered through the windshield at the dilapidated, lifeless old structure standing quietly in the morning sun. The sounds of Dakota's laughter as he chased Biscuit around the yard were as clear in my mind as they had been over forty years ago. The fragrance of the bright orange and yellow flowers Shelly had planted in the front yard filled my nostrils. Sitting in the silence, reflecting on the time we shared our lives together there so many years ago, I felt as though life was literally being squeezed from my heart.

Pat and I spent the day with David and Suzie. Suzie went to their bedroom and pulled out a box of letters, pictures, and Christmas cards I'd sent them over the years. I told them I'd kept the Christmas cards and letters they'd sent. She showed us spoons and other memorabilia they had collected from their travels. Suzie gave Pat two matching Amish dolls and said she would have her mother make a quilt for her.

We walked out to the barn to look at items they'd marked for a yard sale to be held that weekend. Seeing a black hat sitting on the table, I asked David how much he wanted for it. He picked it up, handed it to me, and told me to keep it as a reminder of him.

We took them out for dinner that evening in our shiny new red Mustang GT. Watching the two of them crawl into the back seat was a sight that makes me smile to this day. Both rather large individuals, it was all they could do to squeeze their portly bodies in the Mustang.

"I don't want to tell you what kind of music to listen to, Bob, but if you like country music turn the radio dial to .... " Suzie said, tapping me on my shoulder.

I thanked her and located the station. "That's the one!" she said, humming along with a Merle Haggard tune. Smiling inwardly, I couldn't help but remember the time Jacob and Fannie caught me listening to my stereo at the farmhouse.

David brought us up to date, saying that Fannie Yoder died shortly after we left the Amish, that Jacob and Katie Beiler left the Amish community a few years after we'd left, and had divorced.

"Mandy's married and has seven children. Emma Yoder married a feller from Indiana and lives there with her husband and family."

We dropped them off at their farmhouse after dinner. Revving up the Mustang's powerful engine, I put the transmission into first gear.

"How fast will it go Bob?" David yelled out.

"140!" I shouted back.

"You always did like to go fast!" he laughed, as we pulled away.

Epilogue

So now I sit in front of my desk, trying to put my feelings on paper. Peeling back the layers of my past, I allow myself to remember, and relive, the good and the bad times: reflecting on what was, and what could have been.

The changes that occurred as a result of living with the Amish have had an everlasting impact on my life. I often find myself looking at the world through "Amish eyes," remembering how simple and innocent the world was back then, and how protected and secure I felt.

Even now, I miss my Amish family, and find myself longing for the days when I got caught playing my stereo, winding up in an overturned porta-potty in small town America, racing Eli in our horse-drawn buggies over a bumpy rural dirt lane, helping a family raise a barn, and the night I rescued Tanner from a violent thunderstorm.

Could I give up my worldly goods and return to the simple, idyllic lifestyle of the Old Order Amish? Back to a world where black-garbed, bearded men plow their fields behind teams of draft horses, and bonneted women hang hand-washed clothes on lines to dry? To a world where families hold barn raisings, and teenage boys in horse drawn-buggies attend singings to choose their brides to be?

I have often wondered.

For as I watch the evening news, and learn of yet another senseless killing, hear of the lawlessness and strife in the world, read about what our children are being taught in our public schools, and struggle with my own life, I wonder whether the Amish might have the answers to many of our problems, and quite possibly, the key to true happiness.

I joined the Old Order Amish seeking a better way of life for myself and my family, and fell in love with a people, and a way of life--a life of humility, simplicity, and hard work. I cherish the bonds I made with my Amish family, and will forever hold dear the time I spent with these very special people, for that very brief moment in time.

About the Author

Bob Brawley, winner of a national contest for his article, *Memories of Route 66,* has ventured into the writing world with his memoir, *Adopted by the Amish: A Family's Pilgrimage Back in Time*. Bob, a retired municipal administrator, lives in beautiful Sedona, Arizona, with his wife, Patricia, and their two terriers, Duke and Lily.

Lightning Source UK Ltd.
Milton Keynes UK
UKHW012343010522
402310UK00001B/97

9 781489 711359